DOCTRINE AND EVANGELISM

DOCTRINE AND EVANGELISM

by
VINCENT TAYLOR, D.D.

WIPF & STOCK · Eugene, Oregon

Wipf and Stock Publishers
199 W 8th Ave, Suite 3
Eugene, OR 97401

Doctrine and Evangelism
By Taylor, Vincent
Copyright©1953 Epworth Press
ISBN 13: 978-1-60608-718-3
Publication date 5/1/2009
Previously published by Epworth Press, 1953

PREFACE

THE TWENTY sections in this book first appeared in a series of articles in the *Methodist Recorder*, and I wish to express my gratitude to the Managing Editor of that journal for permission to reproduce them. With very few changes, the essays are now printed in their original form. Anyone who has attempted to express his ideas on a great doctrinal theme in eight hundred words will realize how difficult such an undertaking is: it would have been much easier to write longer essays. The articles were written in the first place for groups and for individual readers who are interested in the work of Evangelism, which, in the belief of the writer, is one of the first duties of the Christian Church. Although written for Methodist readers, the essays are not denominational in spirit or in intention; they give expression to the Catholic Faith of the Church, to which Methodism, along with other communions in the Body of Christ, is committed. The book is published in the hope that it may help others to commend the Gospel to an age which is wistfully interested in the things of Christ, but which needs to understand more fully the things we preach. It discusses questions on which we must make up our minds before we address 'the outsider'. Precisely how to present the doctrines to others is the preacher's special task, and a difficult task it is; but there can be no doubt at all that the themes here presented and discussed are of first importance in the present age. In this persuasion this book has been compiled and is now sent forth on a wider mission.

VINCENT TAYLOR

WESLEY COLLEGE
HEADINGLEY

CONTENTS

ONE

DOCTRINE AND EVANGELISM

WHAT IS Evangelism? Evangelism is often defined as if it were a special art, the work of leading men to decide for Christ in response to a fervent appeal. There is truth in this way of putting the matter, but it is a very depressing definition for many. It fixes attention upon what *we* do, and easily persuades us to say that we have no special gifts for the task and dislike the technique. It is, of course, the Holy Spirit who leads men to decide for Christ. Our part is subordinate to His, but none the less important.

I would prefer to define Evangelism as preaching the Gospel with the aim, through the Spirit, of seeking a response. The desire for a response is vital, since otherwise we are only teaching or lecturing; and it is fully in accord with Apostolic practice, as it is illustrated, for example, in Acts 3¹⁹: 'Repent you therefore, and turn again, that your sins may be blotted out, that so there may come seasons of refreshing from the presence of the Lord.' It is also significant that this way of understanding Evangelism sets an immediate emphasis on doctrine. Peter's appeal arose naturally out of his doctrinal preaching.

But what is doctrine? Doctrine, as I understand it, is nothing more or less than the content of the Christian message in the thought of our day. Paul and John are doctrinal just because they present the Gospel in this manner. To us their teaching sometimes seems archaic— the Pauline use of legal terminology and the Johannine use of the term *Logos*, the Word; but only a little study

shows us that they spoke the language of their time. I am
not sure that I should like to separate too sharply doctrine
from theology. But the two are not quite the same.
Theology is the *ordered* treatment of doctrine; it raises the
more ultimate aspects of the faith and invites us to study
the history of Christian thought. I do not believe that our
congregations mind an occasional excursion into the
realms of theology, but I am sure they will welcome expo-
sitions of doctrine—not tedious arguments, but telling
testimonies about the nature of Christian truth. They
want to know what the faith is, and it is the business of
preachers to tell them, plainly, tersely, effectively.

What, it may be asked, does doctrine include?

Consider, first, belief in God. Why do we believe in
Him? Can we tell someone who questions us in the office
or workshop tomorrow? Have we any reply to the blatant
atheism of our day? As preachers we are simply ineffective
unless we have definite teaching to give on this matter. It
is not a question of repeating the hoary arguments of the
Middle Ages, which I am far from admitting to be useless,
but of explaining the compelling reasons which lead *us* to
believe in God. I would say the same concerning the
question of authority in Christian belief. We know where
a Roman Catholic looks for his authority and where a
Fundamentalist finds it. Where does a Methodist, or
indeed any Evangelical Christian, find it?

All kinds of questions crowd upon the mind. What is
the image of God in which man was created? What is sin?
What is salvation? What is the significance of Christ?
Wherein does the wonder of His Incarnation consist?
What is the meaning of His atoning death? What is His
ministry on high? Who is the Holy Spirit and what is His
work? What is the importance of the Trinity? What are
repentance, faith, grace, justification, sanctification, the
Church, the sacraments, and the life everlasting? All these

are evangelical topics; they have electric power, so that in considering them men are compelled to take a decision as God confronts them in the manifold operations of His grace.

I often wonder what congregations think of the preaching they so patiently endure. I am sure every preacher needs to abase himself before God. We are too anecdotal, too peripheral, too limited in our range. Alas! the hungry sheep look up and are not fed. We have sorrowfully to confess that some at least have ceased to hear us because they get so little from us. How different it might be if we would preach the faith!

The other day I went to hear an old student of mine. He conducted the service with all the dignity and the beauty which the colleges of today demand. But what would the sermon be? When he announced his text there fell on the congregation that wistful silence of which every preacher is conscious at times, for it was this: 'I determined not to know anything among you, save Jesus Christ, and him crucified' (1 Corinthians 2^2). I could see the congregation looking up, like plants turning to the sun. And yet the substance was simple, but unmistakably direct. The preacher gave three reasons why Paul came to this decision. And the points went home. I have no doubt that hearers went away with these points stamped upon their minds, facing again the deathless appeal of the Cross. That was doctrinal preaching, and it was evangelistic preaching, too.

Dare I make practical suggestions? It would be a good thing if once every three years preachers wrote a short essay for no eye save their own on 'My Gospel'. How clearly this would mark our growth in thirty years! And how certainly it would provide a nucleus for our preaching! I think also we should aim at a terse, direct style, blue-pencilling the unessential, and studying the wonder of words. Did not Winston Churchill write his earlier speeches as many as six times? And above all, I think that we should preach our doctrines feelingly, even passionately, and this not as a matter of art (God forbid!), but because we are possessed by them. And will stewards help us? The Presbyterian elder leaves his minister alone ten minutes before the service—alone with God. What a difference it might make if we had time to dwell on some of Charles Wesley's moving lines.

> *Thou art wisdom, power, and love,*
> *And all Thou art is mine.*

I close where I began—with Evangelism. It is a challenging fact that almost all the great evangelical movements in the Church, from the earliest times, have been doctrinal. The exceptions are few, and some of these, on examination, disappear. Was not the message of St Francis of Assisi charged with doctrine? As surely as the sun rises men will be won—if we preach the Word. Not all indeed, as Isaiah 6[9] and John 12[37] remind us; but far more than we think. The seed falling into good earth brings forth thirtyfold, sixtyfold, a hundredfold.

TWO

WHY WE BELIEVE IN GOD

IN THESE days when doubt and uncertainty are wide-spread, it is important that we should be able to answer this question. Our own faith will be stronger if we know *why* we believe in God, and our testimony to others will be more convincing. Who knows? Someone else might be provoked to say: 'Why, then, don't *I* believe in Him?'

I begin with a dash of cold water. We cannot demonstrate the existence of God. We can only give sufficient reasons why we believe that He has made Himself known to us. God is not the conclusion of a syllogism, but the triumphant object of testimony. There are times, especially when we meet with foolish statements, when we need to resort to arguments; but the main business of a Christian is to testify, to say why we address God as 'Thou'.

The great Schoolmen of the Middle Ages thought that the existence of God could be proved, quite apart from revelation, and many people think so still. But if we look closely at the classical arguments, we shall find that they silently assume that which it is intended to prove. The conclusions themselves spring from richer spiritual knowledge. This statement sounds disappointing, for we would like to smash our opponents on the anvil of debate. On reflection, however, we see that to try to do this reduces God to the level of a proposition or classes Him with historical persons like Napoleon or Muhammad. That is why the Bible takes for granted the existence of God, and why Jesus assumed it, too.

Just a glance at the classical arguments. They are interesting. The 'cosmological argument' affirms that the world had a beginning, and therefore a cause, that this cause must be intelligent and personal, and is, in fact, God. The 'teleological argument' reaches the same conclusion from the evidences of design in nature. The 'moral argument' dwells upon the significance of conscience, moral rewards and punishments, and 'the law written in the heart'. The three are crowned by the subtle 'ontological argument' advanced by St Anselm. The very idea of a perfect Being, he held, involves His existence, since otherwise we could conceive of someone greater. What these celebrated arguments point to is the probable existence of a First Great Cause, an Eternal Designer, a Moral Governor, the Final Reality; but the claim that these names designate the Living God depends on spiritual factors which make faith a worthy venture.

It is far better to ask why, in point of fact, we do believe in God, and then, in the light of the answers, to reconsider the famous arguments.

First, let us be candid enough to say that we believe in God because our parents and teachers believed in Him. We drew breath in a God-filled atmosphere. We saw God in the lives of those we loved. We found Him in the fellowship of a living Church. Of course, it is not good enough for us to base our belief on these considerations alone. Who would want to believe only because his father believed? Nevertheless, the fact is important. We are the heirs of a great spiritual tradition.

Secondly, we believe in God because of the testimony of Scripture. Everywhere the Bible tells of the living God; it speaks of Him in the movements of world history and in the experience of psalmists, prophets, teachers, and apostles. This second point is not merely an extension of the first. The more we steep ourselves in the teaching of Scripture, the more we recognize that it is a supreme religious authority. We believe, not because of the proof-texts it contains, but because through it the Spirit of God warns and teaches us.

Thirdly, we believe because of the teaching of Christ. He does not debate, but reveals His knowledge of the Father and the Father's knowledge of Himself, and declares that He will make known the Father to us (Luke 10^{22}). It is not true to say that Jesus never argues, for He says: 'If God doth so clothe the grass in the field, which today is, and tomorrow is cast into the oven; how much more shall he clothe you, O you of little faith?' (Luke 12^{28}). Even here, however, He quietly assumes the existence of God, and makes it His aim to assure us of the Father's loving care for us. Who has greater insight than He?

Fourthly, we believe because of Christ Himself. Dramatically the Fourth Evangelist represents this truth in the saying: 'He that hath seen me hath seen the Father' (John 14^9). We look at His manger and His cross, His passion and resurrection, and we find that He is the perfect revelation of God.

Fifthly, we believe in God because of the illumination of the Spirit. From Him we receive the inner witness, whereby we cry: 'Abba, Father.' And because others receive the witness, too, we know that we are not self-deceived. One thinks of the great speech of Alexander Whyte at Edinburgh to two thousand angry men deeply moved by the legal decision against the Free Church of Scotland. Describing the scene in the House of Lords, Whyte said: 'Men asked, "How is Rainy taking it?" and the answer was "As smiling as ever". And why? Because he has been long years rooted in God.'

These, then, are some of the reasons why we believe in God. They give the right approach to the arguments I mentioned at the outset especially if we interpret *revelation*, not merely as unveiling, but in terms of current theology, as God's doing, God's activity. He confronts us in Christ; but He also speaks through the stars and in the voice of conscience, although sin and the opaque medium obscure His words. When we find Him in Christ, we find Him everywhere.

Our testimonies are not atomic bombs to blast unbelievers. Indeed, much that we say will be utterly strange because it has to be found true in experience. But, when uttered, testimonies make men think. I should find it difficult myself to resist the thrust that their atheistic assumptions are feebler than mine, that one cannot sensibly believe that the universe began with chance, and that moral good does not explain itself. Yet I know that if men are to believe, they must approach God humbly. They will not be won by repartee. They may have been denied early religious training and lack knowledge of the Bible; but they can look to Christ and open their hearts to the Spirit. Let them listen and know. We know, not because we are more discerning, but because in God's goodness we have felt and seen. Can we not testify, and so be God's evangelists?

THREE

AUTHORITY AND BELIEF

'B Y WHAT authority do you *do* these things? or who gave you this authority to do these things?' Such was the question asked of Jesus in the temple by the chief priests, the scribes, and the elders. One could wish that this question were hurled at us; but, in the circumstances of today, the challenge addressed to us is rather 'By what authority do you *believe* these things?', 'these things' being the Christian faith.

It is disconcerting to find that we can more easily answer this question when it concerns others. The Roman Catholic believes because he obeys the voice of the living Church. If the Church, speaking through the Pope, bids him believe that the Virgin Mary was carried bodily up into heaven, he believes this stupendous miracle. The Fundamentalist finds his final authority in the Bible. If the Bible says this or that, it must be right. There is nothing more to be said. The Quaker believes because he is directed by the Inner Light, although not always on this ground alone. In these answers there is certainly something attractive. If we can accept them, we gain immediate peace. We no longer flounder. Authority has spoken and, like the soldier under military discipline, it is ours simply to obey. No wonder Rome makes converts. It is all so simple, once we have admitted that the Church cannot err.

But why do Anglicans, Methodists, Baptists, Congregationalists believe? No doubt individuals will stress one point more than another, but the basic answer, which I shall try to develop in the present essay, is that we have no *external* infallibility at all. We believe because of the concurrent witness of the Church, the Bible, and the testimony of the Holy Spirit. Belief is our free response to this threefold witness.

I state all this at the outset rather baldly, and, of course, in what follows I must explain the answer more fully; but it is just as well to state the position in its nakedness at the beginning. When we have done this, we can take up the points involved one by one.

Do we really want *external* infallibility? Does a real man, or a real woman, want it? If we do, believing has no meaning, except as an inconsistency. Belief is venture; it is trust; it is the leap of the soul which grasps the unseen. As the Epistle to the Hebrews puts it: 'Now faith is the *titledeeds* of things hoped for, the *assurance* of things not seen' (Hebrews 11¹). It is relying, for good reasons, on what you cannot demonstrate by any spiritual mathematics whatever. Now I do not say that Romanists do not believe, or that Fundamentalists do not believe. What I do say is that they do not believe on the basis of their professed external authority. If your final authority is an ecclesiastical statement, or a book, you accept it, with the feeling: 'That's that.' You cannot believe, in the New Testament sense of that great word, on such a basis. You merely acquiesce in something asserted.

Why do I underline the word 'external'? Partly because the infallibilities I have described are external, but more because there is in Christian experience an *internal* infallibility. This statement seems obscure, but it is really quite simple. Let me explain it.

When the Holy Spirit witnesses to us that we are born of God (see Romans 8¹⁶), we *know* that the testimony is true. The witness is certain.

What we have felt and seen
With confidence we tell,
And publish to the sons of men
The signs infallible.

Precisely! The signs are infallible to *us*. And we do well to publish our discovery to others. But the infallibility is *internal*. It is ours, and that of any man who receives it. But, when publishing it, we cannot say, 'Here is something you must believe, or be damned,' for men will reply, quite honestly from their point of view, although to us it will be ridiculous, 'You are mad'; or, more politely: 'You are self-deceived.' That is to say, what is an *internal* infallibility to us is not *external* infallibility to them. And the same results will follow, if we testify to the historic witness of the Church, and the telling testimony of Holy Scripture. There are no external infallibilities. Thank God!

What, then, is our authority in believing? I return to the statement I made at the beginning. Our authority is threefold.

First, our authority is the living voice of the Church. It does not follow that, because we do not believe in the infallibility of the Pope, the Church has no note of authority. Quite the contrary! Surely, a witness extending over nineteen centuries, the voice of saints, prophets, apostles, and martyrs, means everything to us. If our opinions are at variance with the basic message of the Church, in her creeds and her preaching, there is something wrong with them. The authority is not like that of Magna Carta; it is dynamic.

Secondly, our authority is the living voice of the Bible. Because we do not believe that the world was created in six literal days, we do not dismiss the spiritual authority of the author of Genesis, Isaiah, Jeremiah, of St Paul, St

B

John, and the other writers of the Old and New Testaments. Again, quite the contrary! Our beliefs lack assurance if we lack the insight of the Bible. The authority is not that of a legal deed, but of a chorus.

Thirdly, our authority is the inner testimony of the Holy Spirit. I have spoken of this above, and will only add that it is final for us or it is nothing.

Fourthly, our authority is the *combined* witness of the Church, the Bible, and the Spirit. Where the three agree, why do we hesitate to believe? Throughout, authority is spiritual, and there can be none greater. We can believe only if we are free to disbelieve. That is how Almighty God has made us in the wonder of His grace. He has not seen fit to confront us with inescapable proofs; He challenges us to believe. He gives us planes, an atmosphere, and motive power, but He expects us to use the starter, and to make the venture. Had He given us infallible props, He would have treated us as slaves. He prefers sons, and sons must be free to rise on wings of dauntless faith. We are supported adequately, but not guaranteed. Like everything else in the Gospel, even authority is of grace. It is a gift which does not degrade our nature, but honours us as men.

FOUR

THE DIVINE IMAGE IN MAN

IN AN ELOQUENT passage of great beauty John Howe, the Puritan divine, describes the sad state of fallen man. God, he says, has withdrawn Himself and left His temple desolate. 'The stately ruins are visible to every eye that bear in their front (yet extant) this doleful inscription: "*Here God once dwelt*".' The lamps are extinguished, the altar is overthrown, the golden candlestick is displaced. As in the ruined palace of some great prince, we see here the fragments of a noble pillar, there the shattered pieces of some curious imagery, all lying neglected and useless among heaps of dirt. 'The faded glory,' he writes, 'the darkness, the disorder, the impurity, the decayed state in all respects of this temple, too plainly show the Great Inhabitant is gone.'

This message, from Howe's *Living Temple*, aptly introduces the question for discussion in the present article. Is there a divine image in man? Is it obliterated by sin, or can we still see traces of its presence? There is perhaps no question of greater importance, not only for the theologian but also for the statesman, the educationist, the social worker, and the evangelist. It affects international policy, our attitude to education, our efforts for the Welfare State, our preaching of the Gospel. The doctrine of man is basic.

Thirty years ago we should have dismissed Howe's picture with indignation. With justice we should have protested that 'the Great Inhabitant' has not gone, and we should probably have declaimed Shakespeare's noble description of man. Today we still maintain our protest, but, with

Belsen, Korea, and the Mau Mau in mind, we are ready to see more of truth in Howe's picture than we dreamed possible. Modern psychology disturbs our optimism. It is less easy to quote Shakespeare when we remember Freud. These reflections bring home to us the necessity of second thoughts on the subject of God's image in man.

The phrase, 'the divine image', takes us back to the familiar Genesis story, and especially to the words, 'Let us make man in our image, after our likeness' (Genesis 1²⁶), and the statement, 'And God created man in his own image, in the image of God created he him' (Genesis 1²⁷).

By now we ought to have outgrown the childish objection that this story is only a myth. What is a myth, in this connexion, but a story which in the language of picture tells us truth concerning God, man, and the universe? Literature gives us no nobler and truer description of man than this old-world story. It affirms that it was God's purpose to shape man after the likeness of Himself and that He has done this very thing. The seal of God is stamped on the nature of man. He bears the image and likeness of God. In the language of the Psalmist, he was made 'but little lower than God' and crowned 'with glory and honour' (Psalm 8⁵). This claim is breath-taking in its significance. We cannot affirm anything less, if we take the Bible as our supreme religious authority. But how does it square with science and with our knowledge of man as we see him today?

The modern Christian is foolish if he imagines that his conception of primitive man can be more than a matter of reverent speculation. The claim, sometimes made in the past, that the first man possessed the wisdom of Socrates, the intellect of Aristotle, and the eloquence of Demosthenes is moonshine. All the evidence, which anthropologists have assembled from rocks and fossils is against such suppositions, and there is nothing in Scripture to warrant them.

On the other hand, we may read with suspicion so-called scientific accounts of primitive man as nothing more than a creature of low cunning barely distinguishable from the beasts. What the Christian has a right to believe is that, however humble the origins of man may have been, it was the divine intention that, at a point in his evolution when he could truly be called 'a man', he should have a nature capable of God-like growth in understanding, intelligence, conscience and love. All the possibilities of the divine likeness were present. In man God saw Himself reflected as in a mirror, a pin-point of heavenly light meant to glow into the brightness of a flame. This is what God sought and intended. His purposes for man were utterly and entirely good.

It is the universal conviction of Christians that God's intention for man was frustrated by sin; and this conviction accounts for the various forms of the doctrine of the Fall. The vital issue, in its bearing on evangelism, is the question: 'How far does man, as we know him today, possess still traces of the divine image?'

Some theologians have held that the divine image in man is totally lost. Many who have used the word 'totally', and Calvin in particular, do not mean that the image is obliterated, but that sin has infected every part of human nature. Be this as it may, we must insist that the image, battered and defaced by sin, can still be seen. How can we be evangelists on any other belief than this? And how else can we explain the facts of life? Good in things evil, self-sacrifice in apparently worthless men, conscience crying in the hearts of the godless—how do we account for these things? How shall our theology find room for the depraved man who gives up his place on a raft for another, or who dares death in the mine to rescue comrades?

Not by the easy-going view that man is not so bad after all; but by the belief that the Spirit of the Living God still haunts the ruined temple, still visits the up-turned altar, still stands behind the broken pillars. All this, in the language of picture, is that great doctrine of 'prevenient grace' which meant so much to Wesley, and which we must never forget when we confront men with the Christian challenge. We preach the Gospel because we believe that God never leaves man unvisited, but intends him to be conformed to the image of His Son, Jesus Christ our Lord. The tarnished image in man is refaced, restored, burnished until it reflects the face of Christ.

FIVE

SIN

O NLY A VERY light-hearted optimist can doubt that the world is out of joint. Dr Joad has told us that he was compelled to examine the Christian claim afresh by the manifest presence of evil in the universe. Today our best hopes for human good are repeatedly mocked, so that civilization itself seems under a curse. Sardonic laughter drowns the silvery bells of hope.

It is part of the realism of Christianity that it faces ugly facts. It explains social frustration and the divided heart of man by its doctrine of sin. Longing for the Welfare State and the peaceful friendship of nations, it has no confidence in schemes for human betterment which ignore sin. Sin, it affirms, is the cause of man's woe; it is the cancer of society. The basic fact about modern man is that he is a sinner. It is in this persuasion that I propose to ask in this article, 'What are sins?', and, to go deeper, 'What is sin?' No doubt the distinction sounds like a theological puzzle, but I believe it to be vital. It is because we do not think it out, that our gospel often lacks the clarion note.

Sins are actions. In the last analysis they are acts of rebellion against God, but at first sight we do not see them as such because our sense of God is so faint. We think of them as the infringements of a moral code; as thefts, murders, adulteries. Or we go a stage deeper and describe them as breaches of the law of love, acts of backbiting, malice, pride, and uncharitableness.

This is a much truer description of sins, but we have not

taken the decisive step until we see them in their Godward aspect. It is this aspect which distinguishes sins from faults, mistakes, and crimes. A fault is a defect, but not necessarily a sin; it is an offence against an exact standard of fact or good taste. A mistake is regrettable, but it may be made in good faith. A crime is a breach of civil law, although, of course, it may be much more.

Sins, on the contrary, are offences against God, deeds of treason. We have not really seen them as they are until we have assessed them in the revealing light of a Holy God. Then it is that we understand what the Psalmist meant when, with pardonable exaggeration he said, 'Against thee, thee only, have I sinned, and done that which is evil in thy sight' (Psalm 51[4]), and why St Paul is described in 1 Timothy 1[1-5] as the chief of sinners.

It is manifest that this conception of the nature of sins cannot be brought home to the man who has little or no knowledge of God. He simply cannot understand it. He thinks we are talking nonsense. In these circumstances mere assertion on our part is useless, indeed, harmful. There is only one thing to do—so to present God to men, so to preach Christ, that, enlightened by the Holy Spirit, they will see their sins as they really are. We all have to find the truth of spiritual things when light breaks upon us on the way to Damascus (see Acts 9[3]). It is the Spirit who convicts the world of sin (John 16[8]). Even then a truly awakened man may have to walk a long time on the way of life before he discovers the truth of the lines:

> *And they who fain would serve Thee best*
> *Are conscious most of wrong within.*

There is, however, one thing we can do. We can explain, first to ourselves and then to others, the difference between sin and sins. This distinction is not subtle, for it can be confirmed by knowledge of the human heart. When we perceive it, we are at least prepared to see the true nature of sins, and we are no longer affronted by what preachers declare them to be. What, then, is sin?

Sin is a spiritual condition. It is a state of selfishness which controls and determines our impulses, emotions, and sentiments. It is a condition in which self rules.

This condition is contrary to God's intention. Made in the image of God, man fulfils his divine destiny only when God is the standard of his thinking and acting. But manifestly, man does not act in this way; his actions are self-regarding. Let us not draw the lines too sharply. Thanks to the work of the Holy Spirit within us, we by no means always think only of ourselves. The mother thinks of her children, and forgets herself; the teacher of his pupils; the citizen of the sick, the unprivileged, and the outcast. Whenever we do these things, we are not, to this extent, in a state of pure sin. God Himself moves within us. All this must be thankfully affirmed. If, however, we desire to see the true nature of sin, we must avoid the deadly peril of self-justification. We must be candid enough to recognize that even our best motives are mixed. Our charity is often self-regarding, our altruism marred by selfishness. Herein lies the very essence of sin as the Bible understands it.

To see sin aright we must see it when it is full grown. It is self-coronation, wearing God's crown, carrying His sceptre, bearing His orb, mounting His throne. It is like banditry, it is spiritual piracy. It is the soul's proud boast: 'We will not have Thee to reign over us.' No doubt this is sin in its acutest form, and there are all kinds of gradations in it from Hitlerism to a deadly kind of 'respectability' like that of the Pharisee who thanked God that he was not as the rest of men. Only so long as we can say, 'God be merciful to me a sinner', and mean it, can we go down to our house 'justified rather than the other' (Luke 18¹⁴). Such is sin. Its importance is that it is out of sin that sins arise. Our sins are acts of rebellion against God because we have taken His throne.

It may be objected that the Christian view of sin is grim and forbidding. Grim it is, but because the facts are grim, and because Christianity is too realistic to flatter human nature. But is it really forbidding? Its darkness reveals the shining glory of salvation. The analysis does not end in pessimism. It is the background of a great gospel. Against the dark clouds stands the Cross, the only means of dethroning self, banishing sin, and restoring to man the broken image of God, the only final cure of the world's ills, the one means of reconciling man to God, and therefore men to men.

SIX

SALVATION

HANDEL'S script writer was surely inspired when he began his script with 'Comfort ye, comfort ye, My people', and then continued with the Air, 'Every valley shall be exalted', and the Chorus, 'And the glory of the Lord shall be revealed'; for Christianity is essentially a gospel of salvation.

This broad emphasis it shares with other religions. Buddhism and certain forms of Hinduism are doctrines of salvation, however different they may be from Christianity. The same emphasis can be seen in political programmes. The politician claims to be able to deliver men from social and economic evils; and, to this extent, his programme is a message of salvation. It would be wrong to think of Christianity as though it had nothing to do with these evils, for social problems and international issues belong to its doctrine of salvation. Man must be saved corporately as well as individually. Nevertheless, the distinctive element in the Christian message is that it goes deeper, to the root cause of all man's woe—his selfishness, pride, and anxiety, his conscious or unconfessed desire to wear God's crown. Christian salvation is deliverance from sin, restoration to fellowship with God, and the attainment of perfect love in personal and corporate relationships. No lesser definition will serve.

To St Paul salvation includes even the universe itself. The world, he says, was subjected to vanity 'in hope that the creation itself also shall be delivered from the bondage of corruption into the liberty of the glory of the children of

God' (Romans 8²¹). In Ephesians, that climax of Pauline teaching, God's purpose is 'to sum up all things in Christ, the things in the heavens, and the things upon the earth' (Ephesians 1¹⁰). There is no grander, more comprehensive message than that of salvation, and no vocation greater than that of making it known. Three things need to be emphasised. Salvation is the work of God; it is accomplished in Christ; and it is received by faith.

First, Salvation is of God. No other view is possible, if we take the Bible as our authority, sealed by the historic witness of the Church and the testimony of Christian experience.

The historians, prophets, and psalmists of the Old Testament never ceased to present God as a redeeming God. Significantly enough, they saw this truth in His *activity*, especially in the deliverance from Egypt and from Babylon. With reference to the Exodus, Deuteronomy 6²¹ says: 'We were Pharaoh's bondmen in Egypt; and the Lord brought us out of Egypt with a mighty hand'; and in Isaiah 40⁹ the prophet of the Exile cries: 'O thou that tellest good tidings to Jerusalem, lift up thy voice with strength; lift it up, be not afraid; say unto the cities of Judah, Behold, your God!' The point is that the Return is God's salvation. Again, with great daring, Isaiah 63⁸⁻⁹ pictures God saying to Himself, 'Surely, they are my people, children that will not deal falsely', and then adds: 'So he was their saviour. In all their affliction he was afflicted, and the angel of his presence saved them.' One simply does not know where to stop in recording this teaching. Let anyone to whom it is strange open his Bible and see the redeeming God who blots out transgressions like a thick cloud. And, with new notes, the same teaching rings out in the New Testament. The gift of Jesus is the fulfilment of God's age-long redemptive purpose. 'In

Christ, God was reconciling the world to himself' (2 Corinthians 5¹⁹). He 'commends *his own love* toward us, in that, while we were yet sinners, Christ died for us' (Romans 5⁸).

To see this great truth, that God alone saves, is to receive a light from heaven, but to accept it is often hard. Man wants to save himself, to build his own world, to be the architect of his salvation. Poor fool! The brave walls he builds fall down upon him, he is buried by his own bricks, cut by his own implements. But he gets up again and again, unable to believe that the first step to his salvation is to cry: 'O wretched man that I am! who shall deliver me out of the body of this death?' (Romans 7²⁴). God alone is Saviour. We have to be bruised, beaten, and bludgeoned, until we learn just that. The beginning of salvation is despair.

Secondly, salvation is wrought through Christ. Already, in quoting the New Testament, I have illustrated this teaching. When St Paul cries, 'Who shall deliver me?' he immediately answers: 'I thank God through Jesus Christ our Lord.' It was in this persuasion that the first Christians carried over to Him from the Old Testament the name 'Saviour', and spoke of Him as 'the Saviour of the World' (John 4⁴²; 1 John 4¹⁴). This, they saw, was the meaning of His name 'Jesus', which is 'He who is God's salvation'. So St Matthew wrote: 'Thou shalt call his name Jesus, for it is he that shall save his people from their sins' (Matthew 1²¹). It is interesting to trace the use of the name 'Saviour' in the New Testament. It appears only twice in the Gospels, twice in the Acts, and twice in St Paul. Then comes the flood, but only in the latest books of the New Testament. The reason is that the name was applied in the Greek world to the mystery-gods and to the Roman Emperors. Horror at pagan usage had to be overcome before Christians applied it to Christ, and said, in effect: 'He, and He alone, is the Saviour.'

How Jesus saves demands a study of His person and work, such as will be attempted in later essays in this series. Here, it must be sufficient to say that He alone brings us to God, creates a new centre in our hearts, and renews us daily by His Spirit. He saves us by what He has done *for us* and is *to us* still.

Thirdly, we are saved by faith. This, too, is a truth which will need to be explained. Even now, in the light of what I have previously said, its significance, as dependence upon Christ, can be seen. If the essence of sin is self-coronation, to be delivered from it we must give our allegiance to another; if it is banditry, we must find the true heart's king; if it is piracy, we must haul down the Jolly Roger, and break the flag of Christ. Even this we cannot do by our own power. We have to learn the truth of Ephesians 2^8: 'For by grace have you been saved through faith; and that not of yourselves: *it is the gift of God*: not of works, lest any man should boast.' God has no favourites and no patrons. He draws us all in His own time (John 6^{44}), and when He constrains us, we believe and are saved; fully, when we partake daily of His Spirit.

SEVEN

GRACE

IF WE HAD been living in Athens in pre-Christian days, we should have used the Greek word *charis* quite differently from St Paul's usage when he speaks of 'the *grace* of our Lord Jesus Christ'. We should have used the word to describe the *charm* of a lady, the *grace* of a speech, or the *favour* of a king, but not, as St Paul uses it, to describe the free, unmerited, love of God, active on our behalf. It was the knowledge of Christ, and especially the significance of His Cross, which poured new meaning into the word. Lifted out of the worlds of polite speech and public affairs, it has become a basic conception of the Christian religion, describing, as it does, all the wealth of love which God has poured out upon us in Christ and all the spiritual blessings which come to us in Him.

Curiously enough, we do not find this richer meaning in the first three Gospels. Matthew and Mark never use the word, and Luke has it in the sense of 'favour' or 'thanks'. 'Thou hast found favour with God' is the message of Gabriel to Mary (Luke 1³⁰). Jesus 'advanced . . . in favour with God and men' says the Evangelist (Luke 2⁵²). He also tells us that the hearers in the synagogue at Nazareth marvelled, as they listened to Jesus, 'at the words of grace which proceeded out of his mouth' (Luke 4²²). Even in the Fourth Gospel the word, with the richer meaning appears only in the Prologue (John 1¹⁴, ¹⁶, ¹⁷). Clearly, it was when Christians looked back upon Christ's death and resurrection that the word took on a richer and more glowing colour. 'For of his fulness', writes St John, 'we all received, and grace for grace. For the law was given by Moses; grace and truth came by Jesus Christ' (John 1¹⁶, ¹⁷).

Let me supply illustrations from St Paul; only a few, for there are so many. We all remember the salutations and benedictions in his letters: 'Grace to you and peace from God our Father and the Lord Jesus Christ' (Romans 1⁷, etc.); 'The grace of the Lord Jesus be with you all' (1 Corinthians 16²³, etc.). And again we recall such words and phrases as 'being justified freely by his grace' (Romans 3²⁴), 'You are not under the law, but under grace' (Romans 6¹⁴), 'By the grace of God I am what I am' (1 Corinthians 15¹⁰), 'You know the grace of our Lord Jesus Christ, that, though he was rich, yet for your sakes he became poor, that you through his poverty might become rich' (2 Corinthians 8⁹). It is by grace, he declares, that we have been saved (Ephesians 2⁵). He speaks of falling away from grace (Galatians 5⁴), and of being 'partakers with me of grace' (Philippians 1⁷). All these passages, and many more, can be studied with the greatest profit in that beautiful and rewarding book of Dr James Moffatt, *Grace in the New Testament*. And, of course, other examples, too, in the rest of the Epistles, Hebrews, and the Apocalypse. What better theme, and what better text-book, is there for a Bible class! And is there not a great need to do this, if Dr Moffatt is right in saying that today, inside the Church as well as outside, there are those to whom the word 'grace' in connexion with religion fails to suggest anything real to their minds.

I have chosen to speak of grace at this point in the series because it is only in the light of it that we can profitably study the work and the person of Christ and can appreciate the Christian meaning of justification, forgiveness, reconciliation, and sanctification. Grace is not a mysterious fluid imparted to selected individuals by ecclesiastical rites; nor is it magical power communicated through the sacraments. It is Love active for our salvation; not any sort of love, but Love of God Himself. The Swedish theologian, Anders Nygren, described this Love as 'groundless', 'spontaneous', and 'unmotivated' (see *Agape and Eros*, translated by P. S. Watson, Part II, Vol. I, p. 35). Dreadful words, you may say; but they are worth pondering. God's Love is 'groundless' in the sense that it is caused by nothing outside Himself; it is 'spontaneous' because it goes forth of itself, like a spring or beam of light; it is 'unmotivated' because it does not depend on the worthiness of those on whom it rests. Mr Watson aptly quotes a great saying of Luther in which it is described as

an overflowing love, welling forth from within out of the heart like a fresh streamlet or brook which ever flows on and cannot be stopped or dried up or fail, which says: 'I love thee, not because thou art good or bad, for I draw my love not from thy goodness as from an alien spring, but from mine own well-spring—namely, from the Word, which is engrafted into my heart.'

It is no use taking a step further in Christian doctrine until we have at least glimpsed the nature of this Love, for it is this Love, and this Love only, which is God's Grace.

How does God's Grace manifest itself? There can be no more important doctrinal question. It manifests itself in all His dealings with us, in the doors He opens for us, and in the doors He shuts. Often it appears in His judgements on men and nations, for it can be a tornado as well as a zephyr. Even here Love rides upon the whirlwind and at its peaceful centre there is mercy. It was this perception which led Alexander Whyte, in the great speech to which I referred in an earlier essay, to describe the judgement

c

of the House of Lords against the Free Church of Scotland as 'this vitalizing judgement'. 'My Church', he cried, 'is being made an engine of test, fuller's soap, and a refiner's fire, so that no man can hear of her trial without himself being tested.'

But supremely the Grace of God is made known in Christ. 'The grace of God', writes St Paul, 'was given to you in Christ' (1 Corinthians 1⁴). Grace reigns 'through Jesus Christ our Lord' (Romans 5²¹). This indeed is the perennial message of Christmas, that the Grace of God is manifested to us in the Babe of Bethlehem and in the thorn-crowned Christ of Calvary. Because 'the Word had breath, and wrought with human hands the creed of creeds' we see the wonder of the Grace of God. Without this Gospel what hope have we in life and death? But with it we have everything that matters. 'All things are yours; whether Paul, or Apollos, or Cephas, or the world, or life, or death, or things present, or things to come; all are yours; and you are Christ's; and Christ is God's' (1 Corinthians 3²², ²³).

EIGHT

JESUS

D O WE REALLY believe in the Incarnation of the Son of God? This may seem a strange question to ask immediately after Christmas; but the fact is we do not fully believe that the Word was 'made flesh' (John 1¹⁴) if we think of His humanity as partial and incomplete.

This way of thinking was the earliest of the heresies, that of Docetism, and in the earliest days it took strange forms. Against it St John protested when he wrote: 'For many deceivers are gone forth into the world, even they that confess not that Jesus Christ comes in the flesh' (2 John 7). Some went so far as to say that His body was only a phantom, and even to distinguish between Jesus and Christ. In a strange story in the apocryphal Acts of John, while Jesus hangs upon the Cross, Christ, standing in a cave on the Mount of Olives, says to the Apostle John, 'John, unto the multitude below in Jerusalem I am being crucified and pierced with lances and reeds, and gall and vinegar is given me to drink. But unto thee I speak, and what I speak hear thou.'

This idea appals us. And yet, in wondering how people could ever entertain such a thought, we may easily be guilty of a subtler form of the same heresy if we stumble at the belief that the coming of the Son of God in flesh meant for Him weariness, hunger, thirst, trial, disappointment, fear, the hampering limitations of space, want of knowledge, and restricted power. Luther puts the reality of the Incarnation well when he says: 'He ate, drank, slept, and waked; was weary, sad, joyous; wept, laughed; was hungry, thirsty, cold; sweated, talked, worked, prayed.' In their anxiety to affirm His divinity theologians have sometimes described His humanity as 'impersonal'. Thus, Cyril of Alexandria, when speaking of the day and the hour of which Jesus declared ignorance, was driven to say: 'He usefully pretended not to know.'

Let us look at a contrast. Few of us can bring ourselves to admire the uncouth figure of Epstein's Christ. We are too unsophisticated to say: 'Isn't it wonderful!' We may even call it blasphemy in stone. Nevertheless, it has one un-doubted merit. Epstein makes us see the stark realism of the Incarnation. He says, in effect: 'Forget your pretty lambs, your soft-eyed oxen, your high falutin' talk! Take your creed seriously:

> *Conceived of the Holy Ghost,*
> *Born of the Virgin Mary,*
> *Suffered under Pontius Pilate,*
> *Crucified, dead, buried,*
> *Descended into Hades.*

Mark its sheer objectivity. *He was made man!'*

It must be confessed that loving devotion, with the best of intentions, has obscured this realism; and especially in our modern emphasis on Christmas, with its pictures of the perfect baby, the sweetest of oxen, strong, clean shepherds, and Joseph in his best clothes. The dinky Christmas crib is more reminiscent of Hans Andersen than of the Gospels. We need to ponder afresh the wonder of the fact that Jesus was completely human, knowing pain and disappoint-ment as we know them, cabined and confined by the limitations of humanity, truly man, and indeed *a man*. We must not part with the bread of the Gospel for the pastry of conventional art. In his later years A. E. Whitham was never tired of reminding us of the realism of Christianity. Is this realism of vital importance? I believe that it is, and that is why I am writing in this essay about Jesus of Nazareth.

The New Testament pointedly emphasises the humanity of Jesus. It shows that, unlike the pagan divinities of the Roman Empire, He was born at a definite time and place (Luke 3[1, 2]); it speaks of His parents (Luke 2[27, 33, 41, 43, 48]), and says explicitly that He 'advanced in wisdom and in age, and in favour with God and men' (Luke 2[52]). It mentions His anger (Mark 3[5]), His sleep (Mark 4[38]), His inability to do mighty works when faith was lacking (Mark 6[5, 6]), His compassions (Mark 6[34]). His refusal to give signs (Mark 8[12]), His indignation (Mark 10[14]), His tears (Luke 19[41]), His ignorance concerning the last day (Mark 13[32]), His agony (Luke 22[44]), His cry of desolation (Mark 15[34]). St Paul declares that, for our sakes, He 'became poor' (2 Corinthians 8[9]), and that, although He was in the form of God, He '*emptied himself*, taking the form of a slave, being made in the likeness of men' (Philippians 2[6, 7]). For all its lofty Christology, the Epistle to the Hebrews does not hesitate to mention His 'strong crying and tears', His 'godly fear', and the fact that He 'learned obedience by the things which He suffered' (Hebrews 5[7-10]).

Christians ought never to speak apologetically of these things, or to seek to explain them away, for it is of the greatness of the Gospel that, as Emil Brunner insists, Christ might be mistaken for a mere man, or, as Charles Wesley puts it:

> *He laid His glory by,*
> *   He wrapped Him in our clay,*
> *Unmarked by human eye,*
> *   The latent Godhead lay.*

Why is the humanity of Jesus so important? First, as Jesus Himself taught, true greatness is seen in sacrifice. 'If any man would be first,' He said, 'he shall be last of all, and minister of all' (Mark 9³⁵). 'The Son of Man came, not to be served, but to serve, and to give his life a ransom for many' (Mark 10⁴⁵). He let the light of His Glory die down. He closed it with the dark lantern of His humanity so that its flame was visible only to the eye of faith. He accepted an Incognito, becoming the Unknown whom men might deride, the Stranger on whom they might spit. All this, as that primitive Christian hymn quoted in Philippians 2⁵⁻¹¹ reminds us, was 'the mind of Christ', and it is the mind we are to have also:

> *Thus at his love my love's little candle is lit,*
> *So that at his fire I must melt like wax.*

Secondly, it was essential to His saving ministry that He should completely identify Himself with men. 'That which is not assumed', wrote Gregory of Nazianzus, 'is not healed.' 'It behoved him', says the Epistle to the Hebrews 'in all things to be made like unto his brethren, that he might be a merciful and faithful high priest in things pertaining to God, to make expiation for the sins of the people' (Hebrews 2¹⁷). The sheer humanity of Jesus is not the fancy of a genial liberalism, but the proof of God's grace, the hall mark of divinity, and the indispensable basis of salvation.

NINE

THE SON OF GOD

IN VIEW OF the clamant need for Evangelism, it is not unnatural to feel a certain impatience at the slow rise of the theological building. Are the doctrines I am describing essential to the proclamation of the Gospel? I have not the slightest doubt that they are of crucial importance. Unless the foundations are deeply and truly laid, Evangelism will prove a vain and sentimental enterprise. It is soundly based only if we know who Christ is and what He has done for man's salvation.

If it is fatal to neglect the humanity of Jesus, it is impossible to stop there. Indeed, the greatness of the humanity is not seen, unless it is perceived as the slave form of One who originally was 'in the form of God' and did not regard 'equality with God' as booty to be clutched (Philippians 2⁶). The Gospel is that 'in the fulness of the time God sent forth *His Son*, born of a woman, born under the law' (Galatians 4⁴). The greatness of the stooping is that of the One who stooped. The grace of the humiliation is that it is the humiliation of the Son of God. It is necessary, therefore, to ask. Why do we as Christians affirm the divinity of Christ? and What do we mean by the claim?

With advantage, the second question may be considered first. By the confession that Jesus is the Christ, the Son of God, we do not mean that He is a deified man. We do not mean that, as a reward for His greatness and faithfulness, He was raised to the status of a god, like the Roman Emperor Augustus who styled himself *Divi Filius*, the Son of God. Nor do we mean that He was a divine being created by God, or simply a manifestation of God, the highest and the greatest among men. We do not think it is adequate to say only that He is 'like God'; in short, that He is of like essence with God. All these, and other, propositions were debated in the early Christian centuries, and were rejected as inconsistent with Scripture and the facts of the Christian experience of Christ.

The Catholic doctrine, embodied in the Nicene Creed, is that Christ is 'the Only begotten from the Father'; that is, He is 'from the essence of the Father' and is 'of one essence' with Him. These famous words belong to another world of thought than our own, to the Greek world of the fourth century; but it is a significant fact that statements less precise than these have served only to divide men. It is folly to dismiss these words by the sneer that the Christians of the fourth century quarrelled about the letter *iota*, the difference, that is to say, between *homoousios* (of the same essence) and *homoiousios* (of like essence). A crucial difference turned upon that *iota*. It was the question whether Christ merely resembles God or whether He comes to our world from the depths of God's being. Only the latter conception does justice to the New Testament and the Christian experience of redemption.

What reasons lead Christians to affirm Christ's divinity in the sense defined above? This vital issue must occupy the rest of this article.

First, the words of Jesus Himself are basic. He speaks of Himself as 'the Son' as distinct from 'the Father' (Matthew 11[27]=Luke 10[22]; Mark 13[32]), and uses the name 'Father' in a sense which transcends that familiar to ordinary men (Mark 14[36]; Matthew 15[13]; Luke 22[29], etc.). At His Baptism and Transfiguration He is addressed by the Divine Voice as 'My beloved Son' (Mark 1[11], 9[7]), and His temptations turn on the issue whether He is, or is not, 'the Son of God' (Matthew 4[3, 6]). In the parable of the Wicked Husbandmen He says, with marked emphasis, 'He had one, a beloved son' (Mark 12[6]), manifestly with reference to Himself. He forgives sins (Mark 2[10]; Luke 7[48]), betrays no consciousness of personal sin (cf. John 8[46]), and has an unparalleled sense of filial fellowship with the Father. In the Fourth Gospel this teaching is enhanced, for the writer states his interpretative purpose clearly in the words, 'These are written that you may believe that Jesus is the Christ, the Son of God, and that believing you may have life in his name' (John 20[31]).

Secondly, the testimony of Scripture concerning Jesus is undoubted. St Paul, St John, and the author of Hebrews repeatedly describe Him as 'the Son of God', 'the Son', and 'His Son', although it should be noted, St Paul speaks of Him eight times as often in names already fragrant in Christian worship as 'the Lord', 'the Lord Jesus Christ', and 'Our Lord Jesus Christ'. In a manifesto for the Church at Rome St Paul writes that Christ was 'declared to be the Son of God with power, according to the spirit of holiness, by the resurrection of the dead' (Romans 1[3]). Elsewhere with a note of irony, he writes: 'For though there be that are called gods, whether in heaven or on earth . . . yet to us there is one God, the Father, of whom are all things, and we unto him; and one Lord, Jesus Christ, through whom are all things, and we through him' (1 Corinthians 8[5, 6]). St John identifies Him with the Word, who was in the beginning with God and was divine, and says explicitly, 'And the Word became flesh, and tabernacled among us, and we beheld his glory, glory as of the only begotten from the Father, full of grace and truth' (John 1[14]). And the author of Hebrews, contrasting the ways in which God has spoken in the prophets, says that at the end of these days He has spoken to us 'in a Son', 'the radiance of his glory', 'the express image of his essence', who upholds all things 'by the word of his power' (Hebrews 1[1-3]). All this is but a tithe of the evidence, but it leaves us in no doubt what the New Testament writers thought.

Thirdly, the constant witness of the Church affirms Christ's deity. It is highly significant that in all modern proposals for union it is laid down, without challenge, that the teaching of the Nicene Creed, mentioned above, is fundamental to the life and belief of the Church.

Lastly, the testimony of Christian experience, informed by the Holy Spirit, is that Christ is divine. How else can we account for the forgiveness of sins, the life of faith, reconciliation, and fellowship with Christ? Vital to this confession is personal knowledge of the redeeming work of Christ and the wonder of His risen and exalted life. It is the knowledge that we are redeemed, justified, and sanctified, experiences of communal worship and our participation in the Christian Eucharist, which constrain us to cry, with Thomas, 'My Lord and my God' (John 20[28]). What Christ does reveals who He is, and what He is gives meaning to what He does. Christ's Person and the Atonement cannot be separated.

TEN

THE ATONEMENT

THIS DOCTRINE is absolutely vital. We do not truly see Jesus except in the light of His Cross. We can form no just estimate of what the world owes to Him unless we appreciate His supreme saving work for men. Without this knowledge our trumpet is muted. Our Gospel lacks the ringing note. I consider it, therefore, of essential importance that we should ask again and again, 'What is the Atonement?', even if we never reach an answer which completely and finally satisfies us.

We shall not look for a complete theory in the words of Jesus, but we have the right to expect that He saw a divine purpose and meaning in His Passion and Death. This teaching we find in His sayings. Jesus believed that His mission was to fulfil the destiny of the Suffering Servant of Isaiah 53 who 'bore the sins of many'. Thus, He tried to teach His disciples that He 'must suffer' (see Mark 8³¹, etc.) and that He had come 'to give himself a ransom for many' (Mark 10⁴⁵). On the night in which He was betrayed, He spoke of His blood as 'shed for many', as surrendered life which should establish a new (covenant) relationship between God and man (Mark 14²⁴). He spoke of 'the cup' which He must drink (Mark 10³⁹, 14³⁶), suffered the agony of Gethsemane and endured the final desolation of the Cross (Mark 15³⁴). Manifestly, He believed that His suffering, crowned by the victory of the Resurrection, was the divinely appointed way by which men might be restored to fellowship with God and made to share in the life of His Kingdom.

Fired by the wonder of the Resurrection, the first preachers declared that Jesus had been exalted to the right hand of God to be 'a pioneer and a saviour' (Acts 5[31]). 'Through this man', they said, 'is preached unto you remission of sins' (Acts 13[38]). The exultant belief of the primitive Church was that 'Christ died for our sins' (1 Corinthians 15[3]).

In his letters St Paul develops various aspects of this central truth. He explains that in Christ's death God 'commends his own love' (Romans 5[8]) and sets Him forth as the means of covering sin (Romans 3[25]). He even coins the daring epigram that Christ was 'made to be sin', and immediately adds the words 'that we might become the righteousness of God in him' (2 Corinthians 5[21]). St Peter has the same spiritual emphasis when he writes, 'Christ also suffered for sins once that he might bring us to God' (1 Peter 3[18]). All through his Epistle the writer of Hebrews develops sacrificial ideas, declaring that Christ entered into heaven itself, 'now to appear before the face of God for us' (Hebrews 9[24]). So too St John speaks of Christ as 'the Lamb of God, who takes away the sin of the world' (John 1[29]), and says that God so loved the world that he gave his Only-begotten Son, that whosoever believes in him should not perish, but have eternal life (John 3[16]).

In all this I have only taken cream from the milk of Christian teaching. It is the duty and the privilege of believers, and not of preachers only, to know this teaching and lovingly to trace it in the pages of Holy Writ.

In considering what the doctrine means, it is best to begin by remembering that 'atonement' is 'at-one-ment' or reconciliation. It is deliverance from sin and the gift of life eternal. It is Christ's work *for us* and *in us*. Its precise nature has never been defined by the Church—a fact worth pointing out to the man who says he cannot accept the Church's doctrine of the Cross. All that the Creeds say is that Christ 'suffered under Pontius Pilate', and that He came down from heaven 'for us men, and for our salvation'. Nevertheless, from one generation to another definite teaching has been handed down in worship, art, and music, and, above all, in the Lord's Supper; and in what follows I propose to describe what this teaching is.

First, Christ's death reveals the love of God and kindles in us an answering flame of love. To say this, however, is not enough unless we consider what Christ's love does. If I were sitting on the end of the pier, writes James Denney, and someone jumped into the water, and was drowned, 'to prove his love for me', I should find it quite unintelligible. But, if I had fallen over the pier, and some-one, at the peril of his life, sprang into the water and saved me from death, then I should say, 'Greater love hath no man than this' (*The Death of Christ*, p. 177).

Secondly, Christ bears our sins. As Dr W. R. Maltby puts it, in redemptive love, He betrothes Himself to sinful mankind; and, in so doing, He enters with us into the divine judgement which rests upon sin. This intense experience explains what He meant by 'the Cup' and is implied by His cry of desolation on the Cross. It is mis-taken to describe His experience as 'punishment', for no human judge would knowingly allow one man to be punished for the crime of another. He would say: 'That is unjust.' Although incomparably greater, Christ's Pas-sion is the kind of suffering which even men endure when they deeply love wrong-doers, and it shows that forgiveness is not a light and easy thing. To recognize this truth is to see that the Son of God preserves the divine holiness. It also answers the question of Anselm, 'Hast thou considered how great is the weight of sin?' a question which booms like a bell in the heart of every man who thinks seriously about the Cross.

I should myself go further and say that Christ represents us before the face of His Father. He voices the penitence and shame we so fitfully feel and makes Himself the vehicle of our own approach to God. His Death is the One Sacrifice, by which all sacrifices are superseded, but in which we may share through faith and love, especially when we celebrate the Lord's Supper:

> *My faith would lay her hand*
> *On that meek head of Thine,*
> *While as a penitent I stand,*
> *And here confess my sin.*

Through Christ's deed we are restored to fellowship with God and enter upon the path which leads to perfect love. This act of Christ is not merely an event in a time-series in the past. It is the in-breaking of God's love into history, which gathers up into itself all that is revealed in the past, and reverberates throughout the future, so that it is meaningful now and for all eternity.

This is how I think of the Atonement, and this is how I preach it. I do not say that it is the only way or deny that another man's way may be better. What I do claim is that, unless we can preach the Cross in a worthy manner, we had better not enter upon an evangelical campaign. The only message that has ever stirred the world is that we are undone sinners apart from the Son of God who died for our sins—and takes them away.

ELEVEN

FAITH IN CHRIST

APART FROM faith the Atonement remains outside of us and cannot become a reality in our life. It is a revelation we can receive, but not a saving act on which we can depend. All the more tragic, therefore, is the situation where faith is but half understood and where it means nothing at all. For most people in this country faith is belief in mysterious doctrines, which, it is assumed, have no bearing upon life and conduct. To explain what faith in Christ is, and what it involves, is the primary responsibility of preachers, class leaders, and teachers today, as much as in the days of John Wesley; and no vague prattle about the brotherhood of man or the importance of the supernatural can take its place. What, then, is faith in Christ?

In reply, I propose to mention five points. Faith is not any one of them, but all of them taken together.

First, faith in Christ is personal dependence upon Him. It is self-committal to Him, closing with Him, and cleaving to Him. It is a spiritual venture, in which every part of our nature is engaged—our mind, our feelings, and our will. 'Just as a gull, torn by the gale, comes gently to rest on the shelving rock, so the soul drops its wings, and hides in the breast of God.'

> *Jesu, Lover of my soul,*
> *Let me to Thy bosom fly,*
> *While the nearer waters roll*
> *While the tempest still is high.*

In faith, we cease to trust in ourselves and in our powers, and irremovably rest in Him.

Secondly, this faith is made possible by God. It is futile to think of it as a venture of our own, which we can make at any time, and when we will. We cannot patronize Almighty God. We believe when He draws us, finding it then the most natural thing to do. Faith is our response to His sovereign and constraining grace. This fact illumines many things otherwise strange to us. It explains why the Christian man often feels that his faith is miraculous, almost as if he had nothing to do with it at all. It explains also why we can preach faith in Christ, and for the time being see no response. Men cannot believe simply at our invitation. Faith is evoked by God. All this is no excuse for failing to preach the Gospel, since we cannot know how, and when, God will put forth His hand. A season of revival is one in which He does this. The soul is drawn again home.

Thirdly, faith emerges in the Christian community; it is not only the venture of the individual. It is conditioned by Christian teaching and worship, by the corporate life of the Christian Society, the Blessed company of faithful people. We come to know Christ and to believe in Him through fellowship with other believers. It may be that, in the wonder of God's grace, a man on a desert island will cry, 'I believe', or amid the loneliness of a great city; but normally, we believe because we are nourished. Here lies the tragedy of the neglect of worship and the sacraments and, contrarily, here is the reward of faithful ministry and service. Christians are harbingers, forerunners who await the hour when the bells of God strike. 'And at midnight there was a cry, Behold, the Bridegroom! Come out to meet him.'

Fourthly, the core and content of faith are determined by Christ. Faith is wrought in us; it is not manufactured by us. Its inner nature is determined by all that Christ is and by all that He has done for us. That is why time has been given in these essays to attempt to say who Christ is and what His death means. If Christ is only our Example, or our Teacher, our faith in Him may be lovely, but it is frail; a flower in the teeth of a gale; but, if He is the Son of Almighty God, our Saviour, and our Lord, then faith will be as the flight of an eagle, strong and valiant. Faith feeds on Him in whom it rests. This is why even sceptics by nature may be believers by grace. Faith for them is fashioned by the One in whom they believe. Men venture; Christ sustains. Faith swoops; but Christ is the living rock. It is for this reason that faith can become virile and triumphant. Faith is the title-deeds of things hoped for (Hebrews 1¹); Christ is its builder and security.

Fifthly, and lastly, faith overflows in character and deed. Christian morality is always an overflow and not an achievement. It must be wanted and sought, but it is not the reward of effort. The confession, 'I have tried, and tried, but alas! I have failed', is the cry of Pharisaic morality, the legalism of St Paul before he had lighted upon the secret of 'life in faith'. Few things call for explanation so much as this, both for ourselves and for 'the outsider'. Christians seek the virtues which the best ethical teachers praise, and which, in principle, 'the plain man' commends; but they seek them, or ought to seek them, in another way. The Christian way of morality is different from any other. We are honest, not because honesty is the best policy, but because, through faith in Christ honesty is the law of our mind. We are truthful, not because lying is vicious, but because we believe in Christ who is the Truth. We love, not because love is the queen of virtues,

but because faith in Christ makes love our life. We honour
the claims of social righteousness, not only because hous-
ing, public health, and education are worthy ends; but
because we believe in Him who came that men may
have life, and may have it abundantly (John 10[10]). Full
grown faith is socially combustible; it flames out, and
must do so, in loving deed. It works 'by love' (Galatians
5[6]); and it does so because 'the love of God has been shed
abroad in our hearts by the Holy Spirit, who was given to
us' (Romans 5[5]). Hence the gaiety of the saints, the cour-
age of missionaries, and the grit of social workers!

All this, and more, is faith. If only we had this faith, the
Church would advertise itself. Men would see its fruits
and want to gather them. To offer it to men is our
supreme business, in comparison with which schedules and
bazaars are minor matters. Our commission is not to
invite men to seek a nice mind, so that vice, gambling, and
immorality may be eschewed, but to proclaim a faith
which makes such things impossible because they are
unthinkable.

In Christ, inevitably, we seek a more excellent way.

TWELVE

JUSTIFICATION BY FAITH

A FORBIDDING title! But what of the thing itself? Luther called it 'the article of a standing and falling Church', and John Wesley fully agreed with him. If it has become strange to us, we ought bitterly to repent and seek our first works.

What, then, is Justification by Faith? It is, of course, the central doctrine of St Paul, of the Reformation, and of the Evangelical Revival in the eighteenth century. It ought to be the burden of modern preaching in every pulpit. Every Christian ought to be able to tell his neighbour, in the factory and in the street, what it is.

Justification is the doctrine implicit in two of our Lord's parables, the Prodigal Son and the Pharisee and the Tax-gatherer. When the prodigal returned from the far country he made neither boasts nor claims. He had intended to say, 'Father, I have sinned before heaven and in your sight. I am no more worthy to be called your son. Make me as one of your hired servants.' But he never finished his speech. Half-way through he was interrupted by his father, who said to his servants, 'Bring forth quickly the best robe, and put it on him; and put a ring on his hand, and shoes on his feet; and bring the fatted calf, and kill it, and let us eat, and make merry: for this my son was dead, and is alive again; he was lost, and is found' (Luke 15²²⁻²⁴). This is justification. *It is the doctrine that God does not treat us according to our deserts. He treats us as righteous, when we are repentant sinners, and gives us our standing before Him.* He 'justifies us' by reason of our faith in Him.

It is of the essence of Justification that we can make no claims before God. Jesus mercilessly parodied the spirit of the Pharisee who said, 'God! I thank Thee that I am not as the rest of men, extortioners, unjust, adulterers, or even as this taxgatherer. I fast twice in the week; I give tithes of all that I get' (Luke 18[11, 12]). It is as if we were to say: 'I am not so bad after all, not like some who might be mentioned. I pay my debts; I am a good citizen and a faithful supporter of the Church.'

Jesus exposes the folly of all such claims before God when He says: 'But the taxgatherer, standing afar off, would not so much as lift up his eyes to heaven, but smote his breast, saying, God be merciful to me a sinner.' Still more in His closing comment: 'Truly I tell you, This man went down to his house justified rather than the other; for every one that exalteth himself shall be humbled; but he that humbleth himself shall be exalted.'

But it will be said, 'All this is just the forgiveness of sins. Why did St Paul make it remote by calling it Justification?' Well, it is mainly forgiveness, but it is something more, or, at any rate, it is more than forgiveness as it was understood in St Paul's day. But first note what St Paul says. 'We are justified freely', he writes, 'by his grace' (Romans 3[24]); 'It is God that justifieth' (Romans 8[33]); 'A man is not justified by the works of the law save through faith in Jesus Christ' (Galatians 2[16]); 'Being now justified by his blood' (Romans 5[9]). These are just a few phrases culled from his teaching. We ought to read all that he says. But for the moment these passages will serve. *Summed up in a sentence, St Paul's teaching is that, out of His grace, God puts us right with Himself, not in virtue of our good deeds, but because of our faith in Christ, the Redeemer.* Several questions arise in the mind. Why does the Apostle use the language of the law court? How are we justified 'by faith'? What is the point about Christ's 'blood'? And is not Justification a fiction?

Why does St Paul speak of 'being justified'? If the reader is not interested, he can omit this section; to his loss!

The answer is that in St Paul's day 'forgiveness' meant mainly 'the remission of sins'. Today, thanks to the teaching of Jesus and of St Paul, it means 'broken relations restored'. This explains why he uses the noun 'forgiveness' twice only, and the verb once. (In 2 Corinthians 2[7, 10], 12[13]; Ephesians 4[32]; Colossians 2[13], 3[13], he is forced to use a verb which originally meant 'to show favour'.) What was he to do? He goes to the law courts and finds a new vocabulary. He borrows it from the Jewish belief in a Last Assize.

In the Last Judgement, it was believed, men would be condemned or 'declared right'. Here is a word he can use. He lifts it out of the law court and makes it a word of grace. Without denying the truth of a Last Judgement, he believes that, through faith, men can be 'declared right' here and now; not only at the last day but in the present moment of time. Whence words come doesn't matter; it is the use made of them that counts. When St Paul first used it, 'justification' glittered; today it is as dull as pewter. But why should it be? Why give it back to legalism? The vital question of religion still is: 'How can God, who is of purer eyes than to behold iniquity, accept poor sinners as righteous?' St Paul's answer is: 'Not by works, but by faith.'

But why 'by faith'? I can answer this question only by referring the reader to my previous essay, 'Faith in Christ'. Few today would seriously contend that we are justified 'by works'. And never can we do this if we have brooded on the parables of Jesus, already mentioned, and upon another parable, the Farmer and His Man (Luke 17⁷⁻¹⁰). 'Even so you also, when you shall have done all the things that are commanded you, say, We are unprofitable servants; we have done that which it was our duty to do' (Luke 17¹⁰).

But, again, why 'by faith'? The answer is that faith, as I have defined it, is complete dependence upon Christ; it is ceasing to trust in ourselves, making no claims at all, but resting in Him utterly and completely. 'His blood' is an Old Testament phrase which means His life, freely surrendered in death for our salvation; all that one is entitled to bring under the doctrine of the Atonement. Faith in Christ is not a ticket we thrust across the counter of a celestial bank; it is the identifying of ourselves with all He has done for us. We 'come home' to God trusting to all He has accomplished for us in Christ.

My last question! Is Justification a fiction? When God accepts the sinner as righteous, is He calling black white? Two answers are possible. One is that Justification is of God's mercy. We cannot 'justify' Justification. I respect those who so think, but the answer does not satisfy me. I prefer to say that the moment we cast all props aside, and trust in Christ alone, is the purest, holiest moment in our life heretofore. In that experience we are righteous, to be sure only in germ, and with the whole process of sanctification lying before us. We have a righteous mind, for which we can claim no merit at all. Such is Justification by faith, the open Sesame of the soul to God, the bulwark of freedom, the safeguard against boasting and spiritual pride.

THIRTEEN

SANCTIFICATION

BOTH WITHIN and without the Church many people look upon 'Sanctification' with distaste, if not revulsion. And not without reason! Too many people have claimed to be 'fully sanctified' when all the time it was obvious that they were full of unctuous pride. At the same time, even 'the outsider' believes that followers of Christ ought to be living on a very high plane. When he knows what Sanctification is, he agrees that it is an end we ought to seek, but alas! do not attain. Wesley said that when this doctrine was not preached the work languished. Have we not here the explanation why we so largely fail? We lack saints. We are content with commonplace morality. We droop because we have no wings. We do not even walk on stilts.

Much depends on getting the right word for the Christian ideal. 'Sinless Perfection' or 'Absolute Perfection' will not serve, as Wesley so clearly saw. His own term, 'Perfect Love', is the best available, provided we realize that Perfection is an evergrowing experience, like the perfect bud which opens out into the perfect rose, with ever greater fragrance, richer colour, and finer beauty.

Consider how much Scripture makes of this ideal. The illustrations I shall give are not a tithe of those available. When Jesus was asked what commandment was first of all, He quoted Deuteronomy 6[5], 'Thou shalt love the Lord thy God with all thy heart, and with all thy soul, and with all thy mind, and with all thy strength', adding the command

in Leviticus 19[18]: 'Thou shalt love thy neighbour as
thyself.' 'There is no other commandment', He said,
'greater than these' (Mark 12[31]). In the Fourth Gospel
He says, 'A new commandment I give unto you, that you
love one another; even as I have loved you' (John 13[34]).
'Above all these things', writes St Paul, 'put on love,
which is the bond of perfectness' (Colossians 3[14]), and
again: 'Owe no man anything, save to love one another'
(Romans 13[8]). 'May the God of peace himself', he prays,
'sanctify you wholly; and may your spirit and soul and
body be preserved entire, without blame at the coming of
our Lord Jesus Christ' (1 Thessalonians 5[23]). 'Let us cease
to speak of the first principles of Christ', urges the author
of Hebrews, 'and press on unto perfection' (6[1]). 'Beloved',
writes St John, 'let us love one another: for love is of God;
and every one that loveth is begotten of God, and knoweth
God' (1 John 4[7]). No one can read such passages without
recognizing the tremendous emphasis laid on Christian
attainment.

How did Wesley describe this ideal? 'By Perfection', he
wrote, 'I mean the humble, gentle, patient love of God
and our neighbour, ruling our tempers, words, and
actions.' 'The heaven of heavens', he said, 'is love. There
is nothing higher in religion: there is, in effect, nothing
else; if you look for anything but more love, you are looking wide of the mark, you are getting out of the royal
way. . . . Settle it then in your heart, that from the
moment God has saved you from all sin, you are to
aim at nothing more, but more of that love described
in the thirteenth of the Corinthians. You can go no
higher than this, till you are carried into Abraham's
bosom.' His teaching is enshrined in great hymns, two
of which only can be quoted within the limits of this
essay:

O grant that nothing in my soul
  May dwell but Thy pure love alone;
O may Thy love possess me whole,
  My joy, my treasure, and my crown:
Strange flames far from my heart remove;
My every act, word, thought, be love.

   Refining Fire, go through my heart,
     Illuminate my soul;
   Scatter Thy life through every part,
     And sanctify the whole.

   My steadfast soul, from falling free
     Shall then no longer move;
   But Christ be all the world to me,
     And all my heart be love.

Why, we must ask, has this teaching so largely disappeared? Why is it not the master principle of our religion? How is it that we might even be ignorant of it, were it not so prominent in hymns and in Scripture? The answer, I believe, is that there were inherent defects in the teaching from the beginning, due to the want of adequate theological discussion. These points concern the qualifications it is necessary to make, the doctrine of sin, the time element, and the social implications of Perfect Love.

In what follows I shall attempt, as positively as I can, to present the doctrine as we see it today after two centuries of history and experience. Certain aspects of the teaching stand unimpaired. In particular, Perfect Love is the gift of the Holy Spirit, and is received through faith in Christ exercised moment by moment.

First, the qualifications. From the beginning it was rightly seen that, in this life, Christians are not perfect in knowledge, not free from ignorance and mistake, not immune from infirmities and temptations. But would it not have been better if we had frankly said that Perfect Love can be known in this life only within the limitations of our human existence, which are not ended at death, but require for their surmounting the school of eternity?

Secondly, as regards the manner of the gift Death is the stripping off of limitations, but it cannot in itself make a man perfect. Neither can perfection be imparted instantaneously as a sheer act of divine power. There are high moments of Christian experience, Second and Third Blessings, when the love of God is shed abroad in our hearts by the Holy Spirit who is given to us, but, as Wesley taught, these are preceded and followed by a work of grace within us.

Thirdly, as regards the subtlety of sin. Of this subtlety Wesley often spoke, but when he described Sanctification, he defined sin as a voluntary transgression of a known law. 'If ever sin ceases,' he wrote, 'there must be a last moment of its existence, and a first moment of our deliverance from it.' This statement simplifies the issue too greatly. Sin is not something to be extracted; it is self-centredness, so deceptive that we may not be conscious of it. He who seeks Perfect Love must pray:

> *Show me, as my soul can bear,*
> *The depth of inbred sin;*
> *All the unbelief declare,*
> *The pride that lurks within;*
> *Take me, whom Thyself hast bought,*
> *Bring into captivity,*
> *Every high aspiring thought*
> *That would not stoop to Thee.*

Lastly, Perfect Love by its very nature has the widest social implications. It is not a merely pietistic state, but a strong social dynamic. We thank God for all the social teaching of Wesley, his exposition of the Sermon on the Mount, his condemnation of slavery and war, his active philanthropy, his interest in education, his amazing generosity. But we have sadly to confess that during the Industrial Revolution Methodism lost its way, that too often piety was divorced from social justice, that we have loved God, but not our neighbour as ourselves. For these things the judgement of God has smitten us, and we can but say: 'Righteous art thou, O Lord, and upright are thy judgements.' Happily, we have come to see that Perfect Love transcends class distinctions, the colour bar, and the barriers of nationality. Indeed, it is the only solvent of human woe.

Let us seek nothing less than the gift of Perfect Love, alive to the limitations of ignorance, mistake, and infirmity, alert to the deceitfulness of sin, of pride and vainglory, eager to give to it its widest expressions in service, knowing that here and now we can have that Love, which just because it is perfect will unfold through all eternity.

FOURTEEN

THE HOLY SPIRIT

WHAT DO WE mean by 'the Holy Spirit?' Again and again we read in the New Testament of the Spirit who dwells in men, guides and inspires them. These are divine activities and those of a person. The Holy Spirit, then, is God active in the mind and soul of men, in the world, and in the Church. So much is clear to any one who reads the New Testament.

But immediately we reach this conviction all sorts of questions crowd upon the mind. Who is this Holy Spirit? How are we to distinguish Him from the Father and the Son? These questions are not discussed in the New Testament itself. It distinguishes the three. It does this notably in the Apostolic Benediction, 'The grace of our Lord Jesus Christ, and the love of God, and the fellowship of the Holy Spirit, be with you all' (2 Corinthians 13¹⁴), and again in Ephesians 2¹⁸: 'For through Him (Christ Jesus) we both have access in one Spirit to the Father.'

But three centuries of discussion were to follow before a solution was reached in the doctrine of the Holy Trinity. Something will be said of this later. Meantime, we may claim that it is the only doctrine which gives unity to Christian teaching and experience. It gives us a rich and virile doctrine of God, pulsing with life and power, and providing room for all the blessings which come to us in the fellowship of the Church.

It is wise to begin with the Old Testament. There, as Dr N. H. Snaith has shown us in *The Doctrine of the Holy Spirit* (Headingley Lectures), 'the Spirit of the Lord' is the

power of God whereby men do things which otherwise are
impossible. Literally, the word means 'breath' or 'wind'.
The Spirit of the Lord comes upon Othniel, so that he
judges Israel, and the Spirit is actually said to 'clothe
itself' with Gideon (Judges 3¹⁰, 6³⁴). Specially is the gift
connected with the expected Messianic Age, as we see in
Isaiah 11², 61¹, and Joel 2²⁸. The Spirit is almost personi-
fied in Psalm 139⁷, Isaiah 34¹⁶ and 48¹⁶. ('The Lord God
hath sent me, and His Spirit.')

The first Christians were deeply conscious of being
under the power and direction of the Spirit. It is no
accident that the story of Pentecost is so prominent in
Acts 2. The Epistles of St Paul are full of references to the
Spirit. Men believed that God's ancient promises were
being fulfilled, and in their experience and the life of the
Church they found abundant evidence to confirm their
belief.

Consider what the New Testament writers say. (1) The
Spirit convicts the world of sin, of righteousness, and of
judgement (John 16⁸). (2) He guides men into all the
truth (John 16¹³), and bears witness of Christ (John
15²⁶). (3) Love, joy, peace, longsuffering, kindness, goodness, faithfulness, meekness, and self-control are described
as 'the fruit of the Spirit' (Galatians 5²²). (4) He dwells
in believers, so that it can be said that, if any man lacks
'the Spirit of Christ', he does not belong to Him (Romans
8⁹). (5) He witnesses with our spirit that we are children
of God (Romans 8¹⁶), giving that assurance on which
Wesley laid such emphasis. (6) Both the Christian community and individuals are 'the temple of God' because of
the indwelling Spirit (1 Corinthians 3¹⁶, 6¹⁹). (7) He inter-
cedes for us 'with groanings which cannot be uttered'
(Romans 8²⁶). (8) The Spirit must not be 'quenched' (1
Thessalonians 5¹⁹) nor 'grieved' (Ephesians 4³⁰), since in

Him believers are 'sealed unto the day of redemption'.

I do not pretend that this is a complete summary. Let the reader trace the teaching for himself, or examine it as it is set forth in that fine book by Professor A. L. Humphries, *The Holy Spirit in Faith and Experience*. No one can do this without realizing what mighty resources are at our disposal, how pallid life is without the Spirit, how infinite are the possibilities open to us in Him.

What a problem for Christian thinking! As set forth in Scripture the activities of the Spirit are personal. Not an influence, but a divine person is described. This fact is illustrated in Acts 5[4], where Ananias, charged with lying to the Holy Spirit, is told: 'You have not lied unto men, but unto God.'

The question was bound to arise: 'How could facts be squared with the belief that God is One?' It was impossible to believe in three gods. In some sense, therefore, the three must be one! There are some passages in which the Son and the Spirit appear to be identified. Apparently (although not when rightly interpreted) 2 Corinthians 3[17] is an example: 'Now the Lord is the Spirit.' Moreover, the Spirit is described as 'the Spirit of your Father', 'the Spirit of Christ', and 'the Spirit of Jesus'. But many passages speak of the Spirit as the Father's gift (John 14[26]), or as sent by Christ (John 15[26]), or clearly distinguish the three (Romans 8[16, 17]; 1 Corinthians 6[11], 12[3]; 2 Corinthians 13[14]; Ephesians 2[18]).

If any reader feels that he lacks sufficient oxygen to climb this intellectual Everest, let him at least admit that the problem is very practical. The Fathers and doctors of the Church were not engaged in hair-splitting when they faced it. They were seeking a basis for the experience of

the ordinary believer. No doubt they used Greek philosophical terms. What else could they do? They affirmed
that there are three persons within the unity of the Divine
Being, Father, Son, and Holy Spirit, persons who can be
distinguished but not divided.

Can anything be done to make this doctrine more intelligible for men of today? The philosopher Lotze has given
us a key. 'Perfect Personality', he says, 'is in God only,
to all finite minds *there is allotted but a pale copy thereof*'.
Half our difficulties are due to the delusion that God's
personality is just like our own. Must it not be infinitely
richer? In our personality there is one centre, the self.
May there not be more personal centres in God acting in
perfect harmony, as in the words, 'Even as thou, Father,
art in me, and I in thee' (John 17[21]). The doctrine leaves
us wondering, but adoring. The Schoolmen were indeed
right when they said, 'All things go out in mystery'. The
best way to apprehend the truth is not that of intellectual
subtlety, but knowledge of what the Spirit says to the
churches, what He says to us, and what He does for us.

FIFTEEN

THE EXALTED CHRIST

WHAT IS meant by 'the Ascended and Exalted Christ'? What is the nature of His present activity for us? These are not questions likely to be asked by the outsider, but they are questions which the believer must be able to answer for his own sake and in respect of all his dealings with others.

It must be sorrowfully confessed that for many of us the Exalted Christ means little or nothing. Of Christ within the heart and within His Body the Church we know something. When St Paul speaks of Christ 'in' us, 'the hope of glory', and when St John writes of 'abiding' in Christ, as the branch abides in the vine, the ideas suggested are familiar and meaningful, even though we find it impossible to distinguish between Christ's presence and the activity of the Holy Spirit. But what do we make of the common Christian confession that Christ is 'seated at the right hand of God'? What does Jean Ingelow mean when she asks, 'Art Thou his kinsman now?' or Charles Wesley when he sings:

> *He pleads His passion on the tree,*
> *He shows Himself to God for me,*

and again:

> *Thou didst for all mankind atone,*
> *And standest now before the throne?*

We love the lilt; do we know the meaning?

Of one thing we can be in no doubt. This language is steeped in the teaching of the New Testament. The

author of Hebrews repeatedly quotes his favourite Psalm
110 when speaking of Christ. 'When he had made purifi-
cation for sins', he writes, He 'sat down on the right hand
of the Majesty on high' (1³), and again, 'Of which of the
angels has he said at any time, Sit thou on my right hand,
till I make thine enemies the footstool of thy feet?' (1¹³).
St Paul applies the same Psalm to Christ in Romans 8³⁴
and Colossians 3¹. The first preachers appealed to it (see
Acts 2³³ and 5³¹). What is most important of all, Jesus
quoted Psalm 110¹ in controversy with the scribes (Mark
12³⁵⁻⁷), and said to Caiaphas, 'You will see the Son of
Man sitting at the right hand of power' (Mark 14⁶²).

It is easy to see why this doctrine has suffered eclipse. Its
language belongs to outworn views of the universe. The
Hebrews thought that the world was a flat disc, over-
arched by the heavens like an inverted bowl. Heaven was
up yonder; Hades was down below. If you were exalted,
you went up; if judged, you went down. Modern science
has antiquated such conceptions. But alas! in parting
with them, we have let go the ideas of Christ 'seated at the
right hand of God'.
    Doubtless, if science could give us truer pictorial forms,
we could appreciate the doctrine better. But can it do
this, and has it done this yet? Even scientists themselves
still speak of the sun 'rising' and 'setting', although in fact
it does neither. I suggest, therefore, that we are compelled
to retain the older language, and that no harm at all is
done, provided we know that we are using the speech of
symbol, as when, for example, we quote, 'Orion's studded
belt is dim'. The vital question is what does the language
mean?

First, it means that Christ is *Victor*. The Ascension faith
affirms that His victory is permanent. The imagery meets

E

a modern need. Our peril is that too often we look backward. We revere the inspired Teacher, the great Healer, the patient Sufferer, the crucified Redeemer. We may even think of the Resurrection as an event which happened *lang syne*; and so long ago. Wistfully we peer through the mists and reverence the incomparable Man. This sort of Christianity is not adequate for the needs of today. It will not deliver us from doubt, apathy, and despair. We need to know that sin, evil, and death are broken foes, all the more violent because their time is short. The first Christians believed in *Christus Victor*. So must we.

Secondly, Christ is *Ruler*. He is *Victor et Rex*. He sits upon the throne of God and turns the wrath of man to His praise. He is doing this now. He does it whether men recognize His kingship or not; while evil, at His permission, stalks the earth; when men faint for fear and expectation of the things that are coming on the earth; when the Church is cold and divided in counsel, and we are worldly and proud. 'But now we see *not yet* all things subjected to him. But we behold . . . Jesus, because of the suffering of death, crowned with glory and honour' (Hebrews 2[8, 9]). We cannot demonstrate this to the outsider. It is the challenge Christ makes to our faith. Yet it is not wishful thinking, because it is firmly based upon our knowledge of who Christ is, and what He has done by His Cross and Resurrection. He sits at the right hand of God until His enemies become the footstool of His feet.

Thirdly, Christ is *Helper*. So Stephen found. 'Being full of the Holy Spirit', he 'looked steadfastly into heaven, and saw the glory of God, and Jesus standing on the right hand of God' (Acts 7[55]). His enemies 'saw his face, as it had been the face of an angel'. He looked and was strength-

ened. We have no need to show to the world tired and
beaten faces. We have a Helper, and His help is real in
time of need.

Lastly, the session on high means that Christ is our
Advocate. See 1 John 2¹. This is a belief we have lost in
our haste to be modern. We think we need no Advocate,
having the right of entry into the presence of God. We
say that we want no friend at court to persuade God to
be gracious. But why parody the truth? Christ's inter-
cession is grounded in the deepest needs of our natures
(Romans 8³⁴). We need One who voices our feeble penitence and the dumb, inchoate sorrow of the world; One
who appears 'before the face of God for us' (Hebrews
9²⁴). Christ does this because He is the Son of Man:

> *He hath raised our human nature*
> *To the clouds at God's right hand.*

In worship we praise God for this unceasing ministry;
especially at the Lord's Supper, when we call to mind and
plead His Sacrifice.

These things are ours, and no one can take them away.
They are ours because Christ has not gone into celestial
retreat. He sits at the right hand of God as Victor and
Ruler. He stands as Helper and Advocate. He ceaselessly
strives on our behalf, because He is the same yesterday,
today, and for ever. Pictures? Yes, but blessed be His
name, symbols of eternal realities!

SIXTEEN

THE CHURCH AND THE MINISTRY

IS THE Church of divine appointment, and in what sense is she Christ's Body?

That believers are the Body of Christ is taught by St Paul when he writes, 'Now you are the body of Christ and severally members thereof' (1 Corinthians 12^{27}). The Apostle speaks of his sufferings as 'for his body's sake, which is the church' (Colossians 1^{24}). See also Ephesians 1^{23}, 4^{12}, and 5^{30}. Of Christ it is said that He 'loved the church, and gave himself up for it', in order that He 'might present the church to himself a glorious church, not having spot or wrinkle, nor any such thing but that it should be holy and without blemish' (Ephesians 5$^{25-7}$).

The figure of the body is suggestive; it implies that the Church is the medium through which Christ's mind, love, and activity are expressed in the world. And this significance is greatly increased if we think of the body, not in the Greek sense, as the mere sheath of the soul, but in the Hebraic sense, in which the body may even be the self as the object of thought, 'me' as distinguished from 'I', and as exposed to suffering and sacrifice. As is well known, the body is not the only communal figure by which the Church is described. She is also the Bride of Christ (Revelation 22), the branches of the Vine (John 15), and the flock to which He is Shepherd (John 10 and Hebrews 13^{20}).

The members of the Church are well described by St Paul as 'all that call upon the name of our Lord Jesus Christ in every place' (1 Corinthians 1^2). They include all who confess Christ as Lord and observe the sacraments of His appointing. If the Church had fulfilled the intention of Christ, she would be one throughout the world, not necessarily a single corporate organisation, but a living organism, world wide in extent, apostolic in teaching, united in purpose, and holy in life. No one communion within the Church can justly claim to be this organism. The Body of Christ is a broken Body, alive in its parts, but sundered by sins of disunity, faults of misunderstanding, and grievous schisms. Most communions are conscious of this situation, and one of the most hopeful features of our time is the way in which they are seeking, penitently, to find their true unity in a common devotion to Christ's purposes.

They recite the same creeds, reverence the same Scriptures, and observe the same two sacraments; but they are still perplexed how to find a common mind on questions of order and government, especially in relation to the functions of the Christian Ministry.

How far can the origin of the Church be traced to the mind of Christ? Two well-known sayings (Matthew 16[17-19] and 18[15-20]) expressly speak of 'the Church', but their interpretation is encumbered with difficulty and the first was probably polemical from the beginning. One thing at least is clear. These sayings do not supply any warrant for the more rigid doctrine of Apostolical succession, since, in the promise made to Peter, nothing is said of government within the Church or of the transmission of authority to successors.

Quite apart from these two sayings, the existence of the Blessed Community finds its sanction in many ways: in the choice of disciples commissioned to proclaim the Kingdom of God, in the meaning of the name 'Son of Man', in the teaching of Jesus concerning the New Israel founded by his 'blood of the covenant' (Mark 14[24]), and in many parables and sayings. 'Fear not, little flock', He said, 'for it is your Father's good pleasure to give you the kingdom' (Luke 12[32]). When He spoke of the New Temple which He would establish (Mark 14[58]; John 2[19]), He was thinking of the spiritual house of believers. A communal emphasis, indeed, runs through all His teaching. The very idea of a Kingdom, which is the Rule of God, implies a Community in which that Rule is obeyed. So, too, His teaching concerning cross-bearing (Mark 8[34]) and suffering (Mark 8[31] and parallels), and no less His commands and Beatitudes in the Sermon on the Mount (Matthew 5-7).

What is the Church meant to do? There cannot be any doubt in the mind of anyone who reads his New Testament. She is meant to confess Christ in the world and to maintain unfaltering loyalty to Him. Evangelism is her primary task. She is to go out into all the world, making disciples of all the nations, baptizing them into the name of the Father and the Son and the Holy Spirit, teaching them to observe all the things which Christ commanded (Matthew 28[19, 20]). Her task is to maintain unceasing worship which brings men into the presence of God, to train the weak and the erring, and to beget saints.

Her commission is not political. She has no right to tie herself to any Party programme, although her members, guided by her spirit, are free to pursue political activities. Her task is to bring men face to face with God in Christ and to summon them to His service. All ancillary tasks, the raising of money and social activities within the Church, are secondary, and must always be closely watched lest Churches become benevolent societies or social clubs. It is her duty to speak on questions of wealth, divorce, gambling, and international relationships, not by framing laws and regulations, but by interpreting the mind of the Living Christ. As such, the Church is of essential importance to the life of the world. She is meant to be a city set on a hill.

What must be said, finally, of the Ministry?

Ministers are 'stewards in the household of God and shepherds of His flock'. They are called of God to the ministry of the Word and the Sacraments, and are set aside and ordained for this work by the laying on of hands. Their authority is spiritual and ought to be recognized as such by all the members of the Body. Their task is not that of directing social activities and of raising funds, but that of preaching, teaching, leading in worship, and in the pastoral oversight of old and young. A Church which forgets that these are the primary duties of the Ministry has lost its soul, and a minister who does not remember them in prayer and self-dedication is untrue to his ordination vows.

Few things could contribute more to the growth and well-being of the Church, or could humble its ministers more, than a resolute effort on the part of all the members to free ministers from shackles so that St Paul's exhortation can be fulfilled: 'Take heed to yourselves, and to all the flock, in which the Holy Spirit has made you overseers, to feed the Church of God, which he purchased with the blood of One who is his own' (Acts 20[28]). Lasting revival will tarry until the Church revises its doctrine of the Ministry.

SEVENTEEN

THE SACRAMENTS: BAPTISM

THE TWO Sacraments of Baptism and the Lord's Supper have been celebrated in the Church from the beginning and, apart from the Friends and the Salvation Army, are regarded as of divine appointment and perpetual obligation. This view is set forth in the Model Deed which adds to its statements the phrase, 'of which it is the privilege and duty of members of the Methodist Church to avail themselves'. The injunction is based upon the conviction that the two Sacraments were instituted by Christ and are of supreme importance for Christian worship and life.

The necessity of Baptism is based on Christ's words in Matthew 28[19]: 'Go you therefore, and make disciples of all the nations, baptizing them into the name of the Father and of the Son and of the Holy Spirit.' The use of the triune name in this saying illustrates the form it had come to assume in Matthew's day, for from the Acts of the Apostles we can see that in the first days believers were baptised into the name of Jesus Christ. (See Acts 2[38], 8[16], 10[48].) The name is none the less a legitimate interpretation of the saying. John 3[22] states that Jesus baptized, but John 4[2] explains that the rite was performed by His disciples. The greatest influential factor must have been the fact that Jesus Himself was baptized by John the Baptist (Mark 1[9], etc.)

Lustrations have a long history behind them, especially among the Jews, and were particularly important as regards proselytes, that is, Gentiles who embraced Judaism.

Emersion was felt to be an appropriate sign and symbol of the cleansing power of the Holy Spirit, following upon confession. St Paul sees a parallel to baptism in the death, burial, and resurrection of Christ. 'We were buried with him through baptism', he writes, 'that like as Christ was raised from the dead through the glory of the Father, so we also might walk in newness of life' (Romans 6⁴).

How does Infant Baptism fit into this pattern? We cannot quote any saying of Jesus in which it is enjoined, but from a very early time, and perhaps even from the beginning, it was felt to be in accord with the mind of Him who said, 'Suffer the little children to come unto me; forbid them not: for of such is the kingdom of God' (Mark 10¹⁴). St Paul says that he was circumcized on the eighth day (Philippians 3⁵). Who was to say 'No', if someone asked, 'Why should there not be a parallel rite, symbolizing and effecting the reception of children into the community of the New Israel?' Certainly, we read of whole households being baptized (Acts 16³³), and it is not likely that they were all childless.

Let us not be held by the fallacy about the Baptist baby. Who supposes that the unbaptized child is cut off from the mercy of God? Who imagines that he is unvisited of the Spirit? But to argue that Infant Baptism is therefore un-important is as foolish as it would be to cease to pray for our own children because, alas! there are children for whom nobody prays. And are we to suppose that the Spirit of God can exercise no ministry except when His gifts are *consciously* received? What, then, of intercessory prayer? Many for whom we pray are not aware that they are the objects of prayer; they may not welcome the minis-trations of the Spirit and may even resist them. It is true that such people are conscious beings, but every day the

F

life of the infant is emerging into consciousness, and the gift of the Spirit is not limited to the moment of sprinkling. It is upon all grounds right and fitting that from the beginning, in response to the prayers and faith of believers, the life of the child should be offered to the cleansing and life-giving powers of the Holy Spirit of God.

I have spoken of the work of the Spirit and of reception into the family of God because these are the primary aspects of Infant Baptism. But the act of dedication is important also. This aspect is expressed, perhaps too exclusively, in our existing 'office', but it is of inestimable value. The questions addressed to the parents and to the congregation ought never to be omitted or paraphrased, especially the third: 'Will you give this child access to the worship and teaching of the Church, that so *he* may come to the knowledge of Christ *his* Saviour, and enter into the full fellowship of them that believe?' If such a question is preceded, as it ought to be, by instruction, can the father and the mother ever forget that they said publicly, 'I will, God being my helper'?

The other day I met a very gifted Scotsman who had recently taken his son to be baptized. He had not, I should judge, much personal religion, and his wife was an atheist. But he was not going to deny his child the privilege of baptism. So he held the child, as Presbyterian fathers do, and himself made the solemn promises, for he felt that baptism was of the utmost importance.

Do we feel the same? The day comes when the minister says to the growing boy or girl, 'Will you come to my preparation class for membership?' Do parents realize how much they can help? Can they not say: 'Many years ago now we took you to be baptized. You knew nothing of it, but we believed that it meant a great deal. We dedicated

you to God, and vowed to provide a Christian home for
you. You were received into the family of God, and we
prayed for the gift of the Holy Spirit to rest upon you.
Now that you are being prepared for membership, we
hope that you will come to know what faith in Christ
means, and that so you will complete what was then
begun.'

If these lines meet the eye of any young parents, let me
say, 'The day your baby is baptized is a great day. Greet
it seriously, but gladly. Your baby knows nothing about
it now; but one day it will be different. It is a great thing
to place your child in the hands of Christ, as the women
of Galilee did long ago. Your prayers, faith, and hope will
not be in vain, for you are giving back the child—to God.'

EIGHTEEN

THE SACRAMENTS: THE LORD'S SUPPER

THIS SACRAMENT is variously described as 'the Lord's Supper', 'the Eucharist', and 'the Holy Communion', and is the central element in the Roman 'Mass'. The basic narratives are Mark 14²²⁻⁵ (with parallels in Matthew 26²⁶⁻⁹ and Luke 22¹⁴⁻²⁰) and 1 Corinthians 11²³⁻⁵. The obligation resting upon all followers of Christ to observe the Sacrament is based on the nature of the rite itself and upon the command of Jesus, 'This do in remembrance of me' (Luke 22¹⁹, 1 Corinthians 11²⁴, ²⁵).

No action in Christian worship has done more to preserve the evangelical note in Christianity and to deepen and enrich personal devotion and fellowship in the Church. The great 'words of institution', 'This is my body' and 'This is my blood of the covenant, which is shed for many' (Mark 14²², ²⁴; 1 Corinthians 11²⁴, ²⁵), bring home to us the innermost meaning of the Cross of Christ. As I have said elsewhere, 'The Eucharist falls within the orbit of the Atonement alike by reason of the teaching of Jesus and of the life and experience of the Church' (*Jesus and His Sacrifice*, p. 322).

From the beginning the Lord's Supper has held a central place in the devotional life of 'the people called Methodists'. Richard Green writes: 'Wesley taught his people by precept and his own practice the importance of frequent communion. The Sacrament of the Lord's Supper was administered to the Societies in London every Sabbath Day' (*Wesley Biography*, p. 44). These facts have been made abundantly clear in J. E. Rattenbury's *The Eucharistic Hymns of John and Charles Wesley* (1948) and J. C. Bowmer's *The Sacrament of the Lord's Supper in Early Methodism* (1951). During the middle period of Methodism, in reaction to the Oxford Movement of Pusey and Newman, there was a grievous decline in Methodist practice; but a growing and sustained return to our 'first works' is one of the healthiest signs of today.

What do the words of Jesus mean? 'This is my body' is used with reference to the bread which Jesus broke. It does not imply any change in the substance of the bread, as the doctrine of transubstantiation teaches, for this teaching is based on an outworn philosophy according to which, while the outward appearances (the 'accidents') remain the same, the underlying reality is changed so that, in substance, it becomes what it was not before. Neither do I think that it implies that the bread is a mere symbol. The word of Christ, not the action of a priest, changes its value and significance, so that it becomes a means whereby we receive Christ. Moffatt's translation, 'Take this, it means my body', is well justified, especially if we remember that in Hebrew thinking 'the body' belongs to the personality and can mean 'myself'. In eating we share in the power of Christ's self-offering.

'This is my blood of the covenant, which is shed for many.' These words interpret the wine. It, too, has a new significance given to it by Christ Himself. Four words in the saying need to be explained. First, 'blood' in the Old Testament is the sign and symbol of life (Leviticus 17[11]). Secondly, 'the covenant' describes the lordship of God over obedient men, illustrated in the story of Exodus 24[1-8], where, in fact, the very phrase 'the blood of the covenant' is used. The word suggests also the idea of a 'new

covenant' (Jeremiah 31[31]), expressed in the Pauline form of
the saying: 'This cup is the new covenant in my blood'
(1 Corinthians 11[25]; see also Mark 14[25]). Thirdly, 'shed'
calls to mind the words, 'He poured out his soul unto
death', in Isaiah 53[12]; and, fourthly, the phrase 'for
many' does not mean 'some and not all', but, as Isaiah 53[12]
shows, contrasts the many who are blessed with the one
who suffers for them. If we gather all these ideas together,
we see that the wine is received as a means, and a pledge,
of sharing in the life of Christ poured out in sacrifice on
our behalf.

What, then is the opportunity given to us in the Lord's
Supper? In answering this question, I do not wish to lay
down views binding upon all, but, in Methodist fashion,
to give my own testimony. We have to grow into the
meaning and blessedness of the Lord's Supper, and the
things I shall mention are, as I see them, the privileges
open to us for our discovery and use.

First, the Lord's Supper is a *memorial*; it powerfully
reminds us of all that Christ has done for us, and con-
tinues to do for us. Secondly, it is a *sacramentum*, that is, a
bond or oath of loyalty to Christ, and to one another, in
a common fidelity and obedience. Thirdly, it is a
eucharist, an act of solemn yet joyous thanksgiving, in
which we adore God for His unspeakable gift to us in
Christ. Fourthly, it is an act of *communion* with the Living
Christ which we share with the whole Church of God,
militant and triumphant. Lastly, it is *pleading* and *confession* of the finished work of Christ for the sins of the
world. All these ideas are gathered up for us in the great
words of Charles Wesley:

> *Victim divine, Thy grace we claim,*
> *While thus Thy precious death we show.*

We need not now go up to heaven,
  To bring the long-sought Saviour down;
Thou art to all already given,
  Thou dost even now Thy banquet crown:
To every faithful soul appear,
  And show Thy real presence here.

Here is the heart of Christian worship, including and embracing within itself all that is true of prayer, confession, aspiration, hope, and exultation. To celebrate this loving rite is to climb the Mount of Transfiguration whence, strengthened and renewed, we descend to the plain where men dispute and devils wait to be cast out.

NINETEEN

THE LIFE EVERLASTING

'THE EXPERIMENT will be over, the crystals gone dissolving down the wastepipe.' These words of H. G. Wells, written now long ago, express, I fear, a fairly widespread opinion from which even some Christians are not immune in times of spiritual depression. Not a few echo wistfully the question of Job 14¹⁴: 'If a man die, shall he live again?'

At the moment the tendency in theology is to stake everything on belief in God and communion with Him. Here indeed is the true foundation of life eternal, and I shall return to this point later. I mention it now because it seems to me regrettable that, in consequence, we should neglect thoughts which have sustained faith in the past. Arguments, not conclusive in themselves, may still have great force.

Science is not able to demonstrate the reality of life after death, but its teaching concerning energy and evolution will always be significant to the truly religious mind. Nature, in the annual miracle of spring, with its birds, butterflies, and flowers, has a message which time does not dim. One thinks, for example, of the fine words of John Fiske: 'I believe in the immortality of the soul, not as a demonstrated truth of Science, but as a supreme act of faith in the reasonableness of God's work.'

We need not neglect philosophy because we no longer think, with Plato, that the soul is naturally immortal. Nothing renders foolish the belief that the universe is rational. If so, it is hard to believe that the fabric of life drops finally from the loom with no certainty that the design will be completed. Nor can we ignore the finest intuitions of the poets about 'the chainless soul' with 'its strange powers, and feelings, and desires', which refer to 'some state of life unknown' and prompt the reflection: 'And thus I know that earth is not my sphere.' I can never forget a friend who lamented the passing of a loved one, and then quietly breathed the words of Shelley:

> *Peace, peace! he is not dead, he doth not sleep—*
> *He hath awakened from the dream of life—*
> *'Tis we, who lost in stormy visions, keep*
> *With phantoms an unprofitable strife.*

I am not persuaded that we may think lightly of the injustice of death, the 'world-strangeness' of William Watson, the beliefs of primitive man, the tombs of Uadji and Tutankhamen, the long silent voices of Egypt, Babylon, India, Persia, Greece, and Rome. From all narrowness in theology we should pray to be delivered, for the Light which lightens every man is seen in 'intimations of immortality' the world over.

Nevertheless, when full justice has been done to philosophical and ethical arguments, it remains true that our hope in the life everlasting rests finally upon God's revelation of Himself in His Word and in the Person of Jesus Christ.

It is remarkable how slowly and how late the assurance of life after death arises in the Old Testament. Here the emphasis lies upon the value of the present life (Psalm 102[24]; Proverbs 3[1, 2, 16]), coupled with a fear and dread of death (Psalm 6[4, 5]; Isaiah 38[18]; Job 14[10]). One can see the reason for this when the unattractiveness of the Hebrew conception of the underworld (Sheol) is considered, for Sheol is a region of emptiness and darkness (Job 10²²), peopled with weak and ineffective shades (Isaiah 14¹⁰), and remote from the experience of fellowship with God (Isaiah 38¹⁸). The birth of a better hope came through experiences of suffering, the 'discovery of the individual', and a fuller knowledge of God (Psalm 16⁹, ¹⁰; 49¹⁵; 73²⁴; Daniel 12², ³). To take time to trace out these Scripture references is a rewarding discipline, for it reveals the background against which the teaching of Christ is rightly seen.

Jesus shared with the Pharisees a firm belief in life after death. When questioned by the Sadducees, He put His finger on the vital argument when He spoke of God as the God of Abraham, Isaac, and Jacob, and said: 'He is not the God of the dead, but of the living' (Mark 12²⁷). The reality of communion with God is the assurance of life everlasting. The Fourth Evangelist truly interprets Christ's significance in the words: 'I am the resurrection, and the life: he that believeth on me, though he die, yet shall he live' (John 11²⁵). The first Christians exulted in the belief of life after death, and the basis of their conviction was the resurrection of Christ Himself. 'Now has Christ been raised from the dead', wrote St Paul, 'the firstfruits of them that are asleep' (1 Corinthians 15²⁰), and, arguing from the analogy of the seed and the plant, he declares that 'as we have borne the image of the earthy, we shall also bear the image of the heavenly' (1 Corinthians 15⁴⁹). A later New Testament writer speaks of Christ 'who abolished death, and brought life and incorruption to light through the gospel' (2 Timothy 1¹⁰). Generations of believing Christians have found unspeakable comfort in the words of the Seer John, who heard a voice from heaven saying: 'Write, Blessed are the dead who die in the Lord from henceforth: yea, saith the

Spirit, that they may rest from their labours; for their works follow with them' (Apocalypse 14¹³).

There are, of course, very many questions we wish to ask about life everlasting, but on these matters much is hidden from us. We are sure that heaven is a sphere of service, and not idleness (Apocalypse 22³), that an organ of self-expression richer far than our present body will be given to us (2 Corinthians 5¹⁻¹⁰), and that we shall be blessed with the vision of God (Matthew 5⁸; Apocalypse 22⁴). For the rest we must be content to leave questions concerning the immature, the ignorant, and the impenitent to the mercy and the love of God, assured that the Judge of all the earth will do right (Genesis 18²⁵). One thing above all we must make clear to ourselves and to others. Life everlasting is far more than a matter of reward. It affects all our dealings with men, personal relationships, social questions, business matters, international questions. In all these things it makes all the difference whether men are creatures of a day or sons of eternity. If in this life, taught St Paul, we have only a hope in Christ, and nothing more, we are of all men most pitiable (1 Corinthians 15¹⁹); but if, on the contrary, life is the school of eternity, there is every reason to treat men as persons and not things, every necessity to seek the Kingdom of God, every incentive to work together, every inspiration to seek peace and pursue it. Man's dimensions point to his heritage, for God has stamped eternity upon his heart.

TWENTY

EPILOGUE

IN BRINGING this series of essays to an end I wish to comment on some points of interest and importance connected with it. I have not attempted to cover the whole field of Christian doctrine, but only to treat themes of outstanding interest, and especially as they are related to Evangelism. I have rarely referred to the history of doctrine, in itself a most fascinating and rewarding study, but have concentrated upon the testimony of the Church, the teaching of the Bible, and the facts of the Christian experience. In these we find adequate authority for Christian belief and venture.

How far, it may be wondered, has the importance of Christian doctrine been recognized? And, what is more significant, have its intimate bearings upon Evangelism been perceived? These are the questions I ask myself.

There can be no doubt that considerable numbers of young people are finding a new interest in Christian doctrine. The study groups in various parts of the country are proof of this. Further, I think, many young evangelists are discovering that doctrine is of vital importance. It is not enough to stand on soap-boxes and make frenzied and unsupported appeals to the outsider. Hearers welcome warmth of conviction, but at the same time want sound and solid reasons why they should respond to challenge. Evangelists themselves find their message immeasurably strengthened and their own faith enriched, if they know what they believe and why.

But not all young evangelists feel the importance

doctrine. There are some who think that zeal is better than knowledge, thus completely misconceiving the gift of the Holy Spirit; they give the impression to the outsider that they do not know what they are talking about. The result is that many decisions do not last and people are case-hardened against the appeal of Christianity. The situation is exactly described in the parable of the Sower: 'Other seed fell on rocky ground, where it had not much soil, and immediately it sprang up, since it had no depth of soil; and when the sun arose it was scorched, and since it had no root it withered away' (Mark 4⁵, ⁶). It is not enough to sow the seed; we must dig and till the ground.

Little controversy has arisen concerning the doctrines expounded, with one notable exception—the doctrine of authority in belief. Objections have come from two sides, from those who contend for an infallible Church and from those who want an infallible Bible. It may be recalled that the view set forth in these articles is that there is no one infallible authority, since room must be left for the personal venture of faith, but that there is a full and sufficient basis for external authority in the threefold witness of the Church, the Bible, and the Christian experience.

One reader quoted for me the doctrine of his Church concerning the infallibility of the Pope. Without wishing to attack godly members of that community, I can only say that such teaching has no warrant in Scripture or in reason. No true Christian can fail to be impressed by the historic witness of the Church, nor will he want to deny its authority, provided the authority is not presented as inerrant and therefore binding upon all.

It is intelligible that many Christians, in reaction against the claims of an infallible Church, should want to find a fixed basis for belief in an infallible Book. Young ministers have sometimes found themselves confronted with the question, 'Do you believe the Bible from cover to cover?'; and when they have patiently explained in what sense they do accept its authority, they have been told by their questioners that they have no further use for them. This attitude is surely deplorable.

I hope I have made it plain how highly I esteem the authority of Holy Scripture. The essays are soaked in Scripture teaching. I should not feel happy about formulating any doctrine, unless I could show that it has the sanction of biblical teaching. It is, however, another matter when we are asked to accept the Bible as verbally inspired. I should have thought that long ago we had reached a better view. Verbal inspiration is seen to be impossible when the statement of one Gospel is repeated incorrectly in another Gospel (Compare Mark 6[5, 6] and Matthew 13[58]), when a quotation is assigned to the wrong prophet (see Mark 1[2] and Matthew 27[9]), and an event dated in the days of Abiathar the high priest (Mark 2[26]) when it happened in the time of his father Ahimelech (1 Samuel 21[1-6]). To anyone who has a sound doctrine of inspiration such errors are merely spots on the sun, but they are serious matters for a believer in infallibility. Equally awkward is the fact that our oldest manuscripts often vary in small points of detail in the text. Clearly Scripture was not divinely dictated. The truth of inspiration is that God speaks to us through the ancient writers, but within the compass of their limitations. The treasure is given in earthen vessels.

The statement on doctrine in the Methodist Deed of Union reads as follows: '(1) The doctrines of the evangelical faith, which Methodism has held from the beginning, and still holds, are based upon the divine revelation recorded in the Holy Scriptures. The Methodist Church acknowledges this revelation as the supreme rule of faith and practice. These evangelical doctrines, to which the preachers of the Methodist Church, both Ministers and Laymen, are pledged, are contained in Wesley's *Notes on the New Testament* and the first four volumes of his *Sermons*. (2) The *Notes on the New Testament* and the *Forty-four Sermons* are not intended to impose a system of formal or speculative theology on Methodist preachers, but to set up standards of preaching and belief which should secure loyalty to the fundamental truths of the gospel of redemption, and ensure the continual witness of the Church to the realities of the Christian experience of salvation.'

It is to be noted that this statement speaks of (1) 'the divine revelation recorded in the Holy Scriptures', (2) 'the continual witness of the Church', and (3) 'the realities of the Christian experience of salvation'. Here is the threefold basis of authority, as Methodists understand it, and as I have sought to explain it.

I wish, finally, to insist how essential it is that doctrine should be *absorbed* by meditation and prayer, so that it becomes a determining factor in our life and thought. Doctrine must be part of ourselves. Nothing can be more arid than teaching which is almost entirely intellectual. Doctrines become dead if they do not touch mind, feeling, and will. When they are living, they colour our ways of thinking and determine our personal relationships with others; they become mighty themes for preaching and evangelism; they set the course of history and shape the lives of men.

www.ingramcontent.com/pod-product-compliance
Lightning Source LLC
Chambersburg PA
CBHW071107090426
42737CB00013B/2514